Mazda MX-5

Mazda's Affordable Sports Car for the New Millennium

by Jack K. Yamaguchi and John Dinkel
Photo Essay by Kohmei Hanaoka

CONTENTS

Miata, Mazda MX-5, Mazda's Affordable Sports Car for the New Millennium
by Jack K. Yamaguchi and John Dinkel ©1998 by Ring Ltd.
All rights reserved. Printing in Japan. No part of this book may be used or reproduced, stored in
a retrieval system or transmitted in any other form, or by any means, electronic, mechanical,
photocopying, recording or otherwise, without prior written permission of the publishers. For
information, contact Books Nippan, 1123 Dominguez St., Suite "K" Carson CA 90746

PREFACE

I did not think I could ever own an automobile, let alone a sports car, in my lifetime, when I got my driver's license at the tender age of 16 in a driving-school Datsun, a copy of the immortal Austin Seven. My pessimism, I have found, was shared by many Japanese in the Fifties and Sixties, some of whom have since climbed to the top of the Japanese industrial hill, including a couple of presidents of major manufacturers.

How could a young person who wasn't born with a silver spoon in his mouth drive automobiles? Join them if you can't beat them. The fledgling Japanese industry offered no real cars then; most were crude truck conversions with hand-formed bodiess and no match to powerful, sleek Detroit offerings. So I took the good advice of my English professor: read Shakespeare. However, the Stratford Bard did little good for my daily communication, so I switched to Mickey Spillane who made me conversant in English. I got a job as an interpreter with the U.S.A.F. transportation squadron based smack in the middle of Tokyo. Lo and behold, there were Chevrolets and Buicks of 1950 vintage, Willys Jeeps, Dodge 4x4s and GM 6x6s, mine for the sampling.

But still no personal transportation of my own. If four wheels were two expensive, two would have to do. I was fascinated by BWM flat-twin bikes. They were more automotive in design, and I thought they were mechanically elegant with their oil-tight engines and shaft-drives. They were expensive, too. So I joined them again, that is, the Japanese BMW importer as assistant to the manager, who happened to be a BMW engineer on loan from Munich.

To make a long story short, Herr Rinner got bitten by the racing bug, and wanted to beat Honda in Japan's only major race of the time, held on a treacherous dirt road course. Honda was then readying its assault on the Isle of Man TT race in England, and was shaking down its brand new 4-cylinder racing machine at Asama. Herr Rinner wanted to smash the upstart with a couple of mighty flat-twin Beemers. Curiously, he knew his production R69-based engine could not produce enough power, so he reverted to a very American philosophy:

there is no substitute for cubic inches. He told me to find someone to make a set of oversize cylinder barrels (easier said than done!), preferably aluminum ones with cast iron liners because they had to be affixed to the crankcase by shorter bolts than the stock through-bolts, light weight, therefore, being crucial. I got them produced by a casting process called "Sendite," but fiercely argued against the use of the thin casting. Try that with a power-hungry German. So I quit the job. The bike with my locally secured 700-cc barrels blew up spectacularly during a fast practice run, so my former boss had to settle on a 600-cc motor with stock iron cylinders.

Later, a set of more robust aluminum barrels arrived from Germany complete with Mahle racing pistons, which were passed on to my BMW dealer friend, because by then Herr Rinner had left Japan. We raced a sidecar rig powered by the resurrected 700-cc engine in Japan's first three-wheeler race, and won, handsomely, I might add.

During this BMW tenure, 1 got my first car, a BMW Isetta 250, sort of my Sayonara purchase from the importer. A curious and hugely economical contraption, but some may question its car qualification. An old side-valve Hillman Minx, a VW Beetle in my years in England, a first-generation Corolla and a sophisticated Subaru 1000 followed in subsequent years, but they were all mundane transport.

I was truly impressed by Mr. Honda and his creations, and was happy to make acquaintance of some of Honda's engineers during my short racing career, the beginning of a beautiful friendship, so to speak. A Honda in the family, whatever the number of wheels it may have, I told myself. When Mr. Honda brought out his "S" sports car, first the 500, then 600 and 800, I was ready to buy one. A lightly tuned, used example was available at an affordable price. I took my fiancée for a drive to the beautiful Hakone mountains, where I succumbed to massive oversteer and spun out, fortunately only with a minor dent on the fender. On return to Tokyo, she gave me a firm veto on the car. She did not like the scenery revolving 180 degrees around her.

I had to wait until Mazda brought out the first-generation RX-7 before I got a proper sports car of my own. Actually, I consider myself one of the original (Mazda) rotary club members. When I started to contribute to automotive publications, including *ROAD & TRACK* and the British *MOTOR,* only three Japanese makes were "salable items" to foreign media: Honda for the high expectations derived from its motor cycle racing success and unique technology, Toyota with the exotic 2000GT, the first Japanese car to grace the cover of *ROAD & TRACK,* and Mazda with the Wankel rotary engine. I was always fascinated by the rotary, following its rise, near-fall, and its extraordinary ascent again to outright victory in the 1991 Le Mans 24-hour race for sports cars. The latest-generation RX-7 is alive and well in its home country, in the able hand of Takao Kijima, program manager for sports cars at Mazda. But that's another story.

I remember vividly the reaction of people at Mazda's friendly competitors when the first-generation Miata/MX-5/Eunos Roadster (shortened to "ER" among Japanese enthusiasts, before the popular TV series) appeared. A senior Honda designer confessed, "That's the kind of car we should have built. I bought one." That was during a pre-launch drive of the NSX, with a 911, Ferrari 328 and 300ZX, on the Laguna Seca track (I negotiated a loan with my bank and bought an NSX.).

Nick Fell, British Rover director who led the MGF development, showed me a benchmark chart, saying "I think, if we were really honest, the European industry would recognize that Mazda saw a market opportunity and seized it, creating a sports car, the likes of which had traditionally come from Europe, particularly from England. Our work was, partly anyway, to reclaim our own territory." Indeed, the Europeans have returned to the affordable open sports car scene in force, soon to be followed by Honda and Toyota. Thank heaven, "sports" is safe and lives on with cars, not taken away by a myriad of Utes.

Kuni Ishiwatari, Isuzu executive and former design chief, recognizes in his recent Japanese book on automotive design Mazda's enthusiasm and brilliant product development strategy that created the original Miata.

And now, we have the new MX-5 Miata. In the postwar sports car boom, it was new cars that brought excitement and accelerated the movement. MG launched new models every two or three years, following the pre-war TC: the TD, TF, MGA and MGB, with the Midget nicely filling in the entry niche. Triumph followed up its TR2 success with the TR3 and 4, and Fiat the 1100TV with the 1200, 1500, 124 and 2000, interspersed with such nice lightweights as the 850 Spyder and the X1/9. When their development stagnated, and the latter-day models outlived their time, they disappeared one by one.

Program manager Kijima affirms, "Sports cars must be up-to-date, incorporating the latest technology. They must continuously progress."

My hearty thanks to the sports car people at Mazda in Japan and California, especially senior managing director Tadahiko Takiguchi, Hiroshi Yamamoto, Takao Kijima, Koby Kobayakawa, Tom Matano, and Professor Toshihiko Hirai, the "Still-The-One" program manager of the original Miata.

I have been blessed with a great partner in John Dinkel in two book ventures, the third-generation RX-7 and now the new MX-5 Miata book. Without John's profound knowledge of the automobile, his passion for sports cars and editorship of my Shakespearean/Spillanean English, I couldn't have done it.

I had to repeat my early sports car mistake. I took my wife Haru (the fiancée in the Honda S600) for a ride in a Cobra 427 Carroll Shelby kindly loaned me during our honeymoon in California. The experience must have been a bit too exciting. Then a recent ride in a Viper in wet Tokyo, where she had to get out of the car to pay a toll, did not befriend her to open sports cars. Now, I can make up for all that and thank her enough for her patience with a serene open-air motoring trip in a new Miata.

Jack K. Yamaguchi

When I look back, I'm not sure I could put my finger on the specific event that led me down the path of a life-long passion for sports cars. There were a number of opportunities for me to have taken a wrong turn. For instance, when I graduated from high school, my best friend graduated twice: from school and from a 40 horse VW Beetle to a 1963-1/2 Ford Galaxie 500 powered by the "muther" of all FoMoCo engines, the 425 bhp, 427 cid side-oiler V8, equipped with two enormous fuel-sucking Holley 4-barrels. There wasn't a car in the area, Vettes and Hemis included, that could touch that Ford. That car was an absolute blast to drive.

And my parents? Mention sports car to them and they thought I was talking about another planet. The family 1963 Chevy Biscayne six with automatic was more than enough car for any sane individual, thank-you very much!

But somehow along the way, despite overdosing on some scalding hot Detroit iron, I'd managed to discover *Road & Track* and *Sports Car Graphic* and *Competition Press*. Immersing myself in those publications and reading about the exploits of racing greats such as Dan Gurney, Parnelli Jones, A. J. Foyt, Phil Hill, Stirling Moss, Graham Hill and Jimmy Clark, got me thinking about a very different type of sporting transportation.

I really lusted after the BRG Austin-Healey 3000 like the one with the chrome wire wheels and the snarley-sounding, chrome-tipped pavement-dragging exhaust system driven by the smart-ass kid from the Garden City (read "affluent") side of the tracks. But the Healey was way too rich for my blood. It came down to a choice between an A-H Sprite and a Triumph Spitfire. And the Spitfire won out because of its more modern specifications: windup windows and its technically advanced! swing-axle independent rear suspension.

I had great times driving that car. Every mile was a memory. It forced me to become an auto mechanic. And every time something broke, it helped me understand why the British are famous for a stiff upper lip. Equipped with a roll bar and a set of used Goodyear Blue Streaks it took me to touring schools at

Brigehampton and Lime Rock. Later, in full race rim, it took me to my first SCCA driving school at Waterford Hills, Michigan, where I gained a first-hand appreciation of the value of safety belts and a roll bar... and a lesson in who your real friends are.

A few years later, resurrected with a "new" used body, that 1964 Spitfire tail-gated my wife and me all the way to California on a tow bar attached to my 1996 Plymouth Barracuda Formula S. And with a race engine detuned with only a glass-pack muffler, that Triumph carried me on numerous outings along Pacific Coast Highway between my apartment in Dana Point and the R&T offices in Newport Beach. And never once did that now Chrysler hemi orange Spitfire get pulled over for excessive noise.

Then one day, the hemi drag racing Prestolite Transignitor ignition system, which had fallen off the parts shelves at the Chrysler Woodward Avenue Garage skunk works onto the Spitfire's 1147-cc 4-cylinder engine, gave up the spark.

Finding another became akin to tracking down the Holy Grail. And because the option of converting the ignition from a modern Chrysler racing ignition back to the original system with its suspect generator, points and voltage regulator seemed totally revolting at the time, the Spitfire was retired. Initially, it was relegated to the third garage stall, the one with the manual door. Currently, it resides on the apron outside the garage (covered, of course) because a newer but also rarely driven "collectible" 1973 Toyota Celica ST has usurped its previous place of honor.

Sitting in boxes scattered throughout the garage are all the parts (including that original Lucas ignition system) necessary to get that Spitfire running again. As number one son approaches licensing age (he recently got his driving permit), I sometimes casually suggest that restoring the Spit would make a fun father-son project. His typical retort is, "When I get my license, I want an Audi A4 1.8 turbo."

Occasionally, when the right test car shows up at my doorstep, I drive him to a local off-highway parking lot and teach him what driving with three pedals is all about. Lately, I've noted an expanded vocabulary, which includes phrases such as "5-speed manual," "rack-and-pinion steering," "how fast will it go," and "when do I get to drive it."

I think it's about time to introduce him to the Mazda Miata. Throughout my automotive journalist career I've had opportunities to drive virtually every sports car imaginable. There are lots of memorable ones: the Porsches, the Z-cars, the RX-7s, the Ferraris, the Lambos, the Corvettes. All great cars. Still, I find myself inexorably drawn to affordable sports cars like the Spitfire, the Fiat X1/9, the Toyota MR-2 and the Miata. These are cars with an unbeatable fun-for-the-dollar factor. And of all the sports cars and roadsters available today, there isn't another with the ability to put an ear-splitting grin on my face the way the Miata can.

As anyone who has done it knows, writing a book is hard work. This is the second one I've written in collaboration with Jack Yamaguchi, and I couldn't ask for a more knowledgeable or enthusiastic co-author.

To my family, especially my wife, Leslie, and kids, Meredith and Kevin, thanks for allowing me the hours travelling and locked away behind closed doors that are required to write a book like this.

A special thanks to all my friends at Mazda, both here and in Japan, and especially Koby Kobayakawa, for being the sports car enthusiast and friend that he is.

Sheila and Art: I hope you realize that the Spitfire wasn't as "pointless" as you once thought!

Mom and dad, I love you. And, yes mom, after all these years, I have found it possible to forgive you for crumpling the Spitfire's nose with that 1963 Biscayne and then blaming me for having parked behind the Chevy with a car that was too small for anyone to see!

John Dinkel

MX-5 Miata Driving Impressions

by John Dinkel / Photos by Guy Spangenberg

Several months before the 1999 Mazda MX-5 Miata made an official appearance on American roads, I received a call from Takaharu "Koby" Kobayakawa. Followers of the Mazda marque are sure to recognize Koby as the guiding light behind the last generation RX-7. Since Jack Yamaguchi and I collaborated on a book detailing the development of that great rotary-engine sports car back in 1991, Koby has taken up residence in Irvine, California, as Director in charge of Advanced Engineering and Planning of the consolidated Mazda North American Operations.

"Would you be interested in driving an early Miata prototype to give us some impressions of the direction we're headed?," Koby inquired.

My immediate response was simple, "Where and when?"

A date was set for the following week. We'd meet at the Mazda R&D facility, grab the prototype Miata, a 1997 model, a couple of the Miata's European roadster competitors and then head out for an afternoon of fun on one of the best sports car roads in Southern California, actually, anywhere in the world for that matter, Ortega Highway. I expected the new Miata would be trucked out to our driving site in an enclosed trailer, but no, when I arrived at Mazda, I learned we were going to drive the new model, along with the others, in broad daylight, first to a lunch stop along the way and then out to our Ortega rendezvous! A pretty gutsy move on Mazda's part, realizing at that point in time only the most sketchy of illustrations of the new Miata had appeared in print. How did Mazda propose to hide the MX-5's one impossible-to-overlook new styling feature: exposed headlights?

I needn't have worried. Mazda's California designers had created a bra which totally covered the nose of the new car except for cutouts which exposed just enough of the new headlights to make them appear identical to the combined turn signals/parking lights on the then-current model. I laughed. What a great disguise!

Following a quick lunch, it was off down Ortega Highway. What a great sports car road. The diversity of on- and off-camber turns, the high- and low-speed sections, the pavement changing from smooth to rough to bumpy to broken, the up- and down-hill elevation changes — all combined to create a terrific proving ground for any car's suspension, brakes and steering and for evaluating the overall balance between the vehicle's engine and chassis.

Starting first with the current Miata and then jumping into the prototype to test the back-to-back differences, I immediately noted the revised engine's increased flexibility. This comes as a result of some mild tweaking of the Miata's 1.8-liter twin-cam 4-banger, including a variable-volume intake system (VICS), modified cam timing, less restrictive intake and exhaust ports, a compression ratio that's been bumped up half a point and a knock-control system, which add up to seven more ponies and five more lb-ft of torque. These are hardly earthshattering performance increases, but they make a significant difference in how the new Miata feels and responds. For example, the torque curve has been crafted to provide more torque at low rpm, and corners that would have required a downshift from 5th to 3rd in the previous model are now taken comfortably in 4th.

It took me only one tight corner to sing the praises of the revised suspension tuning. As much as I love the handling of the original Miata, the new one has an even more sporty feel. Much of that is a result of the improvement in linearity of steering response and the precise manner in which the chassis plants itself when the car is tossed into a corner. The previous car has what engineers refer to as "non-linear steering gain off center." What this means is that when a driver inputs, say, 30 degrees of steering lock, the system adds an additional few degrees. When the driver senses this "oversteer," he has to unwind some of the lock he has cranked in to prevent the car from turning-in too sharply. By the way, this is not something you'd notice in normal driving, only when cornering aggressively near the car's limit.

The same is true of the improved cornering stability, which results from some minor but significant suspension changes. The front roll center was dropped about three-quarters of an inch, caster was increased and toe changes are minimized by a revised tie-rod location. At the rear, Mazda chassis engineers have incorporated new shock valving along with a longer stroke.

During hard cornering, these changes impart a more stable, predictable feel to the car, which eliminates the occasional slight nervousness of the previous Miata without detracting from the wonderful seat-of-the-pants feel and responsiveness for which Miatas have always been noted. I discovered I could put the power down sooner when exiting a corner — the rear-end really stays planted — and as a result, I could maintain momentum and speed much more easily and comfortably with the new Miata. Also, during aggressive downhill braking, I found the car's better balance allowed me to brake harder into a corner, without the brakes wanting to lock or the rear end getting darty.

The new Miata's overall balance and the forgiving nature of its chassis don't detract in the least from the car's overall sportiness. To the contrary, these attributes allow a driver to maintain higher overall touring speeds much more easily. And, if anything, the new car is even more "tossable" because it's more comfortable when being driven hard near its limits.

During this ride and drive I had an opportunity to drive both a base 4-cylinder BMW Z3 and a Porsche Boxster. I'll have more to say about these and some of the Miata's other competitors in another chapter. For now let me say the following. Both are fine cars. But the BMW is slower and noisier (especially with the top up) and it feels more like a roadster than a sports car. The Porsche has more power, but it has a much harsher ride without any noticeable cornering advantage versus the Miata, and the quality of the car was not up to my expectations based on dozens of previous Porsches I have driven. And both cars, especially the Boxster, are considerably more expensive.

Nine months later I had an opportunity to spend nearly a week in a 1999 Miata, this time with no camouflage bra to detract from the car's subtle new curves and its distinctive exposed ovoid headlamps. The bright red model you see in the photos was the first of the production Sports model, and I was lucky enough to be one of the first journalists offered an opportunity to spend time behind the wheel.

As I walked around the Miata to study its seductive new lines, I thought about the terrific job Mazda had done in redefining the original Miata concept, a design dating back to 1989. Mazda could have done it very wrong. They could have decided to "reinvent" the affordable open roadster and make it "better" instead of making it true to itself. We'd seen that happen before with the likes of the original 240Z and the 2-seat T-Bird. Mazda could have decided to broaden the appeal of the car to generate increased sales volume. Luckily for those of us who love sports cars, Mazda chose wisely, changing a line here and a curve there, but leaving the basic design intact. In fact, you really need to have the "old" and the "new" sitting side-by-side to really see some of the differences. For example, most people will tell you the taillights of the two cars are identical, but they are not.

I really like the subtle re-sculpturing of the sides, which adds a more muscular look and feel to the car. And the rocker panel cladding, body-color "mud flaps" behind the rear tires and the rear deck spoiler provide an added touch of sportiness to the Sports model. As do the handsome 5-spoke 15-inch, brush-finish alloy wheels shod with aggressive 195/50R15 Michelin Pilot SX radials that do a great job of filling up the Miata's wheelwells.

The biggest styling difference is also the most obvious: the headlight treatment. Out with the awkward oversize pop-up headlights of the past. In with the distinctive ovoid lights with their deep reflective mirrored pockets that add depth, dimension and personality to the front end. It's a happy face with a smiling open grille that reminds me of a much beloved roadster from an earlier era, the Austin-Healey Bugeye Sprite.

Drop down on your knees and take a close look at that integrated front-end spoiler and you'll discover slots at either end for ducting air to the brakes. A nice, functional touch.

Okay, back on your feet. It's time to check out the operation of the convertible top. Here's another place where Mazda could have outsmarted itself. Shouldn't a convertible for the new millennium offer a power top with high-tech electronics and a dozen motors? Er, not really. Especially when the one the Miata had was a model of simplicity. And the new one continues in that tradition. It's still just a matter of releasing two convenient windshield header latches, then pushing the top rearward via the center recessed grip and stowing it behind the seats. But the new top features several enhancements. For one, the rear window is glass with defrosting wires embedded in the glass. The plastic window that would cloud with age is a thing of the past. As is the need to unzip the window before stowing the top.

Now let's walk around to the back. The decklid and rear haunches are bulked up, almost as if the previous model had been sent off to pump iron for six months at the local Gold's Gym. Inside the trunk you'll find a very pleasant surprise: more room! The extra space results from relocating the spare tire and battery under the floor. Now there's enough room to accommodate two golf bags, though I must admit I'm taking Mazda's word for this because I spent my driving time behind the wheel and not on the fairway.

Having a few days instead of a few hours to experience the new Miata only served to reinforce the impressions I had formed from the earlier Ortega Highway drive. What a sweetheart of a sports car. It totally involves you with the driving. Start the engine and your ears are treated to the melodious sounds of a twin-cam engine and a staccato exhaust note that has "sports car" written all over it.

Now move that shift lever into first gear. The gearshift action is as close to a Formula Ford as you'll find in a street-driven production car with throws that are delightfully short and crisp. You'd have to be the all-time "ham fist" to miss a gear. The shifting in the previous Miata was beyond reproach, but this one is better. Changes include a perfectly shaped shift knob and improvements to reduce shift effort and vibration.

It's obvious someone who understands sports cars picked the five ratios in the manual gearbox. They are perfectly matched to the engine's torque and power curves. And the shifting is complemented by pedals that are ideally positioned and weighted for precise heel-and-toe downshifts. Alex Zanardi, here I come!

The Miata's engine/gearbox combination set you on a mission to seek out tight twisty roads. The engine runs eagerly to its 7,000 rpm limit, but its exceptionally strong low- and mid-

range flexibility and perfect gear spacing mean you can short-shift at 4,500-5,000 without missing a beat.

The engine is winding to around 3,200 rpm in top gear at 60 mph — really short gearing in this day and age when a Corvette, for example, loafs along at 1,320 rpm at the same speed. However, I never felt that a 6th gear would have been useful to lower engine noise or reduce stress on the engine.

This was the Sports model of the new Miata which means it's equipped with Bilstein shock absorbers and a front strut tower cross brace, as well as those previously mentioned fat grippy Michelins that generate neck-wrenching cornering power. Precise power-assisted rack-and-pinion steering with exactly the right amounts of quickness, effort and road feel and powerful 4-wheel disc brakes are part of a suspension package that add new meaning to the phrase "perfectly balanced chassis." The combination of aggressive treads and firmer underpinnings endow the chassis with great agility and wonderful responsiveness. The nose turns-in quickly and precisely and the rear sets and sticks, instilling immense confidence in even a neophyte Andretti.

Inside, the Miata features stylish new cockpit contours, a handsome Nardi 3-spoke steering wheel and excellent analog gauges with black backgrounds and white numbers and pointers. The two large dials for the speedometer and tachometer are flanked by a fuel gauge to the left and a coolant temperature gauge to the right. Above and between the tach and speedmeter is the oil pressure gauge.

The seats are comfortable and supportive, but anyone taller

than around six feet two inches will probably wish for a bit more room.

The layout of controls and switches is just about perfect. Lighting functions and wiper/washer operation are controlled by two steering wheel stalks. The radio is now mounted above the climate controls, which operate via simple rotary dials for adjusting temperature, air flow distribution and fan speed.

A covered, lockable center console box contains remote releases for the trunk and the fuel-filler lid. This console area also features two cupholders/stowage areas and a small ashtray directly behind the shifter.

The passenger side of the dash not only contains an airbag with a kill switch but also a large locking glovebox. Larger door map pockets also are useful improvements.

But perhaps the most appreciated improvement is the high level of fit, finish and quality of materials found throughout the interior. The new Miata reeks of new-found quality and refinement. The car feels much more solid than its predecessor with nary a squeak or rattle.

Do I have any gripes? Only one. The Sports model offers no power assist — not for windows, mirrors or door locks. No problem there, because, hey, this is the Sports model. But when I brace my left leg against the door panel when going around hard right-hand corners, the window winder digs into my knee.

What is it about the Miata that makes it such a special automobile? The answer is simple: Fun. Pure unadulterated, wind-in-the-face driving fun. And its honesty. It's a classic, affordable, open-top sports car that doesn't pretend or promise to be anything it isn't. Like a seductress, it beckons you to put on your string-back driving gloves, take the top down, slip behind the wheel and head for your favorite twisty road. You'll rev the engine and you'll relish in the joy of shifting up and down through the gears. You're as one with the road and the world, feeling out your favorite corner as though it were your first time. These are pleasant thoughts and memories.

This is the Miata.

Chapter

1

ANATOMY OF
THE NEW MX-5 MIATA

BODY AND SOUL

The Chicago Auto Show, February 1989, witnessed the rebirth of the affordable, lightweight open sports car in the form of the Mazda Miata. It was subsequently named "Eunos Roadster" in Japan and designated, simply, "MX-5" for elsewhere. Whatever name it carried and wherever it went, the roadster was received warmly, and in many instances enthusiastically, around the world. By the end of November 1997, more than 430,000 cars were delivered, the U.S. taking half of them.

The Miata rekindled a powerful flame among the world's enthusiasts for exhilarating open-air motoring and imparting the joy of "Oneness between the car and driver." The compact open sports car movement was revived and gathered momentum with important new models from Europe's prominent marques such as BMW's U.S.-made Z3, the Rover MGF, the Fiat Barchetta, and in higher price brackets, the Porsche Boxster and the Mercedes SLK.

The Hiroshima-based manufacturer insists that it holds to the belief that a sports car must be thoroughly contemporary and up-to-date, incorporating the latest technological developments. The original MX-5 has thus been constantly refined, including two major updatings and numerous improvements.

Takao Kijima, MX-5 program manager, says, "The last decade of the century has seen giant leaps in technology, particularly electronics, but also in the design and development and manufacturing of the automobile." He continues, "At the same time, society's concern about safety and environmental issues have become more acute."

It was time to move on. Kijima affirms, "There was one fundamental principle guiding Mazda's design and engineering team for the new MX-5's personality. We must value and assert the car's inborn 'Soul,' and train, strengthen and refine the 'Body.' The new car required no conceptual revision: Enhance the virtue of the compact, lightweight two-seat open sports car, and offer a sports car unparalleled in ownership delight and driving pleasure, to people of all walks of life, young and young at heart. We pursued new dimensions in open-air motoring, fun-to-drive and styling."

CONFIGURATION AND PACKAGING

Mazda also focused on new dimensions in dynamics and quality. However, the new Miata's physical dimensions are basically unchanged from the original car. The overall length and height are the same at 155.3 in. (3,945 mm) and 48.4 in. (1,229 mm), respectively. Its width of 66.1 in. (1,680 mm) is only 5 mm wider than the original MX-5.

The wheelbase remains the same at 89.2 in. (2,266 mm), while the front track is increased by 5 mm to 55.7 in. (1,415 mm), and the rear track by 10 mm to 56.7 in. (1,440 mm) when fitted with alloy wheels. The front and rear tracks of the model equipped with steel wheels are 55.3 in. (1,405 mm) and 56.3 in. (1,430 mm), respectively.

A strict diet was imposed on the car's physique for compactness, and lightweight materials were the essential ingredients during the design and development of the new

New MX-5 is similar to the first-generation model in basic configuration with the "front-midships" engine driving the rear wheels. The spare wheel and battery are now placed under the trunk floor.

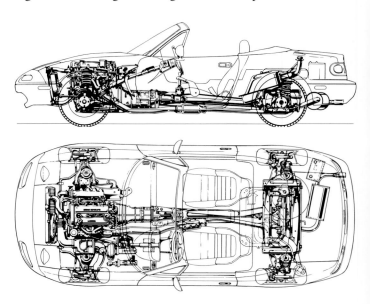

Spare wheel and battery occupied a large part of the trunk in the first-generation Miata.

The power unit and the final drive/mount bracket are united by an aluminum Power Plant Frame (PPF). Suspension is independent by double wishbones.

Miata. The base U.S. Miata weighs 2,299 lb (1,045 kg), a scant 6 lb heavier than the 1994 1.8-liter model, no mean achievement if one considers the latest safety requirements, including a reinforced body and standard dual SRS airbags, plus a more powerful engine and added comfort equipment and accessories. By the way, the original U.S. Miata, powered by a 1.6-liter engine and with the driver-side SRS airbag only, started out at 2,116 lb (960 kg) back in 1989.

The Miata continues with its front-engine, rear-wheel-drive, open-body, two-seat sports car configuration. A low yaw-inertia (polar) moment is critical to a sports car's dynamic performance. Therefore, the mechanical mass is concentrated within the wheelbase with the placement of the engine "front-midship," attaining an ideal 50/50 weight distribution.

For weight reduction as well as moving as much mass closer to the car's center of gravity, those endearing pop-up headlamps are replaced by fixed, flush-fitting lamps integrating the turn signal/auxiliary lights. This alone saves 12 lb (5.6 kg). Also, the bumper system incorporates a novel lightweight blow-formed plastic reinforcement bar at the front and an extruded aluminum bar at the rear, covered by lightweight polypropylene facias.

The new Miata inherits the original model's unique unitary power plant; the power unit and the final drive are united by an aluminum Power Plant Frame (PPF). The power plant assembly is attached to the sturdy front and rear subframes using four rubber mounts. The subframes are in turn bolted to the welded-steel integral body shell.

The four-wheel all-independent suspension is a refined version of the original Miata's unequal-length upper-and-lower arm (classical "double wishbone") design with concentric coil springs, tubular shock absorbers and anti-roll bars. The suspension's spring and shock absorber rates, bushing characteristics and geometry have been recalibrated and optimized with a number of new components for superior handling and roadholding and improved ride quality. Steering is by rack-and-pinion with engine-speed-sensing power assistance on most of the models.

The all-steel, welded integral body is strategically reinforced to ensure optimum noise, vibration and harshness (NVH) control, and to provide maximum occupant protection in case of an accident.

The original Miata had one of the best-engineered-and-built soft tops; light in operation and fairly secure and weatherproof. However, Mazda's designers, engineers and manufacturing technicians set out to outdo themselves in creating a "world-class" convertible top. The soft top now has a glass, heated-element-imprinted rear window that requires no unzipping when folding. Yet, the top is lighter than the previous version, which had a clear plastic window, due to vigorous weight-saving. An optional SMC hardtop is offered, as before. The new soft top can be installed on the original Miata as a replacement unit, and the original car's hardtop can be fitted on the new car.

Although the interior has been redesigned, its vital dimensions and space are basically unchanged. During the redesign, Mazda's layout engineers uncovered useful and precious storage space within the compact body. They were able to relocate the spare wheel and battery into recesses under the trunk floor, increasing the trunk volume from the previous model's awkwardly shaped 4.4 cu ft (124 liters) to 5.1 cu ft (144 liters). Also, the glove compartment volume has been increased, and a number of useful pockets and bins are provided in the interior.

MODEL RANGE

Two engine and three transmission types are specified in the new MX-5 range.

The U.S. Miata is powered by the updated type-BP 1.8-liter 140-bhp (SAE net) engine, available either with an improved version of the type-M15-D 5-speed manual transmission or a new Aisin electronically controlled 4-speed automatic. The California-specification Miata's power is 138 bhp. The European MX-5 is offered with the type-BP 1.8- and type-B6 1.6-liter engines. The B6 was re-introduced in the MX-5 range in Europe in 1994, with its maximum power limited to 90 bhp (EEC rating) to receive a favorable insurance rating. In the new car, its power has been raised to 110 bhp (EEC) because of a change in the insurance rating system. Initially, either engine type is mated to the type-M15M-D 5-speed manual transmission.

The Japanese Mazda Roadster has the most power unit permutations: two engines and three transmissions. The type-BP 1.8 is combined with the new Aisin-Mazda type Y16M-D 6-speed manual transmission with a direct fifth and overdrive sixth. The 1600 is equipped with the 5-speed gearbox. The 4-speed automatic is available in either engine series.

The U.S. Miata and Japanese 1800 are available with a sports suspension with firmer springs, Bilstein shock absorbers and thicker anti-roll bars, combined with 195/50VR15 tires on 15 x 6JJ alloy wheels. In the U.S., it is offered as the Sports Package model, the subject of John Dinkel's road impressions, and in Japan as the 1800RS, which is more comprehensively equipped.

MODEL LINEUP

	U.S.	EUROPE	JAPAN
1800			
BP 1836 cc	s	s	s
5-speed manual	s	s	n/a
6-speed manual	n/a	n/a	s
4-speed automatic	o	n/a	o
Normal suspension	s	s	s
Sports suspension			
(with Bilstein shocks)	o	n/a	o
1600			
B6 1597 cc	n/a	s	s
5-speed manual	n/a	s	s
4-speed automatic	n/a	n/a	o

Note: s = standard
o = optional
n/a = not available

EYES AND MOUTH

"The original MX-5's youthfully contoured and smoothly rounded shape and cheerful countenance (often described as 'cute') won the heart of many a sports car aficionado around the world," says Koichi Hayashi, chief designer of the new MX-5 Miata. His team in Hiroshima, Japan, and those at the company's California design center strove to preserve that adolescent charm, yet have matured the new car's styling to be thoroughly disciplined and refined, appearing more muscular and tauter and conveying strength within.

The face of the Miata is eyes and mouth. In the original car, the eyes were the auxiliary lamp clusters. Now the eyes are open with clear purposes: illuminate the road effectively, and be lighter in weight in the dynamically critical front overhang. The lens and reflector are designed to create a jewel-like impression.

The mouth is friendly as ever, yet more functional, the larger air-intake, with perhaps a hint of seriousness about it, providing better cooling. The sculptured facia/bumper face flows into the car's lower flanks and hood. A separate, small spoiler behind the facia/airdam improves under-floor airflow, and contributes to improved straight-line stability and steering response.

The hood is shaped toward twin peaks formed by it and the top of the fenders. It has a subtle central bulge, a functional necessity to leave, literally, plenty of breathing space for the engine.

The door handle is a new flush-mounted and color-keyed design with functionality as its primary objective (a broken nail could turn a friend into an instant enemy, as Mazda designers have discovered).

The outside mirrors have larger viewing areas, and their housings have a ridge that deflects rain water.

The rear end is readily recognizable as the MX-5 with its characteristic oblong tail-lamp clusters, which wrap around the more prominently tapered body contour. Each cluster houses the tail/brake-, directional signal- and back-up-lamps. The European model also has a rear foglamp integrated in the cluster.

The rear deck repeats the front end's twin peak theme from which it rises to a gentle central hump integrating a high-mount

DIMENSIONS

		U.S. Miata
EXTERIOR		
Wheelbase	in. (mm)	89.2 (2,266)
Track, front	in. (mm)	55.7 (1,415)*
rear	in. (mm)	56.7 (1,440)*
Overall length	in. (mm)	155.3 (3,945)
width	in. (mm)	66.1 (1,680)
height	in. (mm)	48.4 (1,229)
INTERIOR		
Head room		
(with top closed)	in. (mm)	32.9 (835)
Leg room	in. (mm)	42.8 (1,086)
Shoulder room	in. (mm)	49.7 (1,263)
TRUNK		
Volume	cu ft (liters)	5.1 (144)
* With aluminum alloy wheels		

U.S. Sports model is fitted with P195/50VR15 Michelin Pilot SX GT high-performance tires on 15 x 6JJ alloy wheels.

The U.S. Sports model with rear wing.

Japanese base 1600 comes with manual steering and steel wheels. It is primarily aimed at two types of buyers: those who want an inexpensive sports car that "looks" fast with add-on aero-pieces, and those desiring raw material for a sports car they can modify to go fast. The Japanese version is called "Mazda Roadster."

The soft top has an integral glass rear window with heating elements imbedded in the glass.

Right-hand-drive model for export with an optional SMC hardtop. For Europe and elsewhere, the car is called simply "Mazda MX-5," sans Miata.

A ridge on the mirror casing deflects rain water from the mirror face.

A second airdam under the nose improves aerodynamics.

Fixed headlamp with integrated turn-signal lamp.

brakelamp.

An American Appearance Package offers a front airdam extension, side-sill extensions and a rear spoiler-wing. The front airdam and rear spoiler are included in the American Sports Package. All Japanese models, including the 1800RS, can be fitted with these aero pieces.

INTERIOR AND AMENITIES

The MX-5's interior is true to the car's sporting soul and mettle. Mazda designers and engineers focused on refining and improving the interior's function and appeal to three human senses – sight, sound and touch.

The instrument panel reflects the "T-shape" theme, a design element Mazda has cherished and applied to its sports cars, beginning with the Sixties' remarkable twin-rotor rotary-powered Cosmo coupe. The upper part of the instrument panel is softly padded and contains four "eye-ball" adjustable ventilation/heating outlets, another feature of the MX-5's interior theme. The panel houses the standard passenger-side SRS airbag, above the larger glove compartment in the lower dashboard.

The instrument cluster is deeply hooded to avoid reflection, and houses the large speedometer and tachometer, flanked by smaller, round fuel-level and coolant-temperature gauges. Centrally located between the larger meters is an oil-pressure gauge. Warning lamps are placed under the oil pressure gauge. Meter and gauge faces are now in a shade of navy blue instead of the previous black hue, and the white needles contrast more clearly for improved readability. An electronically driven speedometer is adopted to eliminate nervous "twitching" of the needle.

A liquid crystal total/trip mileage display is located between the main meters. The odometer's two functions alternate, and the trip recorder is reset by a single push/turn knob.

A new urethane, four-spoke, 15-in. (380-mm)-diameter steering wheel is standard. The BP 1.8-liter range can be fitted with a stylish three-spoke, leather-wrapped, 14.6-in. (370-mm)-

diameter Nardi steering wheel (standard on the European 1.8). Because the inertia moment of the three-spoke steering wheel is greatly reduced, the driver is provided with a more natural steering feel. Both steering wheels incorporate a driver-side SRS airbag under the center pad.

The lower portion of the central console contains the heating and ventilation system (and the optional air-conditioning), which is controlled by three clearly marked dials, instead of the previous bar and dial controls. An audio unit can be installed above the heating/ventilation control panel. Under the heating/ventilation control panel is a passenger-side SRS airbag deactivation switch and warning lamp panel. A small open cubicle fills this space in the European and Japanese models.

A navigation display, a popular Japanese option, is now integrated within the audio control panel. The 5.6-in. display electrically pops out when in use, and has a split-screen and voice guidance functions.

The one-piece tunnel console contains the shift lever, an ashtray and a lidded oddment storage bin. In the lidded space, folding cup-holders and card slots are newly incorporated. In addition, the size of the locking glove compartment volume has been increased from 0.15 cu ft (4.2 liters) to 0.22 cu ft (6.3 liters).

The door trim includes a gas-injection-formed pull grip, as well as a map pocket. Another useful pocket is provided on the passenger-side seatback, and there is also a mesh pocket on the "Wind Blocker."

The seats are buckets with deep, integral bolsters and head restraints. Many improvements were incorporated to achieve weight reduction, and better support and comfort, even during long trips behind the wheel. The seat design incorporates noise suppression measures including larger slide-rollers, O-rings on the hinges and a urethane insert on the fore-and-aft adjustment lever's return spring. In the U.S. Miata, the seat's central sections are upholstered in new higher-quality, supportive woven cloth material, while the European and Japanese versions have softer moquette textile, the difference being dictated by market preferences.

A tan leather interior package is available in the U.S. Miata and as the 1800VS package in Japan. The latter includes a classic wood-rimmed, three-spoke Nardi steering wheel and a wood shifter knob and a wood brake lever grip.

"Wind Blocker"

The folding Wind-Blocker board is standard on all models, except the U.S. Sport Package (a curious omission!), the Japanese base model and the European 1600 series. It is positioned on the shelf behind the seats. In an open two-seat car, a portion of the air passing over and around the occupants flows back into the cockpit, greatly reducing the heating/air-conditioning system's efficiency as well as ruffling hair. The Wind Blocker prevents air-flow reversal and the turbulence caused by it. The board's shape and height are designed so as not to obstruct rearward vision, and it can be folded down when

U.S. Sports model interior with Nardi leather steering wheel and shifter. In this model, windows are manually wound down and up. A deactivation switch for the passenger-side SRS airbag is standard in the U.S. Miata.

Japanese VS Special two-tone interior with tan leather seats, trim and wood-rimmed steering wheel, wood shifter and brake lever. A tan interior is available in the U.S. Miata, but with a leather Nardi wheel and shift knob.

Right-hand-drive export model with the standard four-spoke steering wheel.

U.S. speedometer is calibrated to 140 mph-plus with smaller metric readings up to 240 km/h.

Japanese 1800's speedometer and tachometer needles rest at six-o'clock position. The speedo reads up to 180 km/h, a voluntary industry restraint.

European speedo goes to 240 km/h.

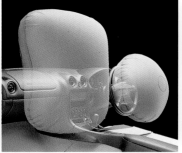
Dual SRS airbags are standard equipment. The driver-side airbag on the U.S. Miata is depowered.

U.S. Sports model's woven cloth bucket seats provide excellent support.

not in use (as with the top in place, or the occupants want to have more wind). It enables open-air motoring in cooler climates.

Bose Premium Audio System

Mazda seems to appreciate fine quality audio systems even — or especially — in its sports cars. Witness the third-generation RX-7's awesome Bose "Bazooka" speaker that robbed most of the already small luggage space, and the previous-generation Miata's "Sensory Sound System," which employed a couple of head-restraint-installed speakers to energize your brain and a seat-back transducer-speaker to kick your back, not to mention

pairs of door-mounted speakers and tweeters.

They have done it again, this time more elegantly and efficiently, courtesy Dr. Amar Bose and his extraordinary sound specialists. In an open sports car, the sound system must overcome road noises emitted during both low- and high-speed runs, a feat a conventional premium audio system may be hard put to cope with. The Miata's Bose® audio system is driven by a pair of ultra-lightweight (700 grams each), switching amplifiers, each putting out maximum 100W, and uses Bose's state-of-the-art Nd™ speaker technology. A neodymium-boron magnet possesses a magnetic density 10 times as powerful as a normal ferrite magnet. This, together with the Nd™ speaker's unique flat helical voice coil construction, enables a very compact outer size. The 8-in. woofer is 1.7 in. thick (43 mm) versus a typical 6 x 9-inch speaker's 3.3 in. (82.7 mm) thickness, neatly fitting into the Miata's door. Two Nd™ speakers are combined with two 2-in. "Extended-range Tweeter" speakers, or "Twiddler" in Bose jargon, also installed in the upper front corner of each door. Unlike the tweeter, which covers a high frequency zone, the Twiddler has a wider range in the mid- and high-frequency sound zones.

New Miata has a number of bins and pockets for oddments; the covered tunnel console holds two cups.

The folding "Wind-Blocker" prevents air-flow reversal into the cockpit.

The head unit, also from Bose, fits in the central console, and consists of an AM/FM radio and a CD player. The head unit incorporates the audio specialist's patented dynamic equalization circuit, which automatically adjusts the system's sound energy balance for faithful and natural reproduction.

The new Bose system answers the Miata engineering team's relentless pursuit of light weight; it saves 13 lb (5.9 kg) compared to the Sensory Sound System.

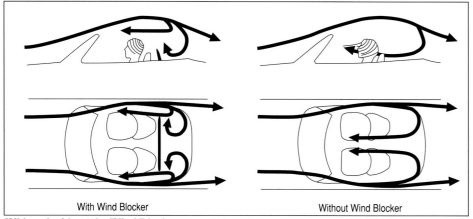

With Wind Blocker   Without Wind Blocker

With and without the Wind Blocker.

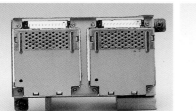

Bose audio system is optional. A compact 100-Watt switching amplifier weighs a scant 700 grams and occupies minimum space. Two amplifiers are used in the system.

Bose's state-of-the-art Nd™ 8-inch woofer and 2-inch "Twiddler" speakers fit neatly in each door.

Navigation systems are popular options in Japan. An optional visual/voice navigation system is integrated into the center console.

Enlarged trunk has 144-liter volume versus the previous model's 124 liters.

ENGINES

The Type BP DOHC 16-Valve 1.8-liter Engine

The primary engine for the new MX-5 is the type BP double-overhead-camshaft, 16-valve, electronically fuel-injected 1839 cc unit with 83.0 mm bore and 85.0 mm stroke. It produces 140 bhp SAE (Society of Automotive Engineers standards) net at 6,500 rpm, which is 7 bhp higher than the previous Miata. Likewise, the maximum torque value of 119 lb-ft at 5,500 rpm is beefier by 5 lb-ft.

Wouldn't our lives be simpler if the automotive world had gotten together and come out with single unified standards for measurements and stuff? "No way," wryly observes a prominent engineer-executive. "If they can't agree on such basic things, as distance, length, mass, and temperature; like miles versus kilometers, feet and inches vs centimeters and millimeters, pounds vs kilograms, and Celsius vs Fahrenheit. Maybe differences are what make us stay competitive!"

Of course, there are different standards of measurement in the engine's output: what equipment and ancillaries should be included, what emission standards it must comply with, politics and bureaucracies. For California and other states where the new Miata satisfies TLEV (transitional low emission vehicle) requirements with specific engine controls and an additional manifold catalytic converter, its outputs are 2 bhp and 2 lb-ft less, the latter produced at lower rpm (5,000 vs 5,500).

For Europe, the BP is rated at 103 kW (kilowatt) EEC at 6,500 rpm and 162 Nm (Newton meter) at yet lower 4,500 rpm, meeting the European Community's Step II emission standards. SAE's official stance is to encourage using these units for power and torque ratings, but even in Europe they still show PS *(Pfedestarke)* and kg-m (kilogram meters). The Japanese favor PS and kg-m, but in its own JIS (Japanese Industrial Standards) units which are not too different from the SAE's. In Japanese tune, the BP puts out 145 PS and 16.6 kg-m at the same rpm as the U.S. version. Then there are such things as the French Ch *(cheval-vapeur)* and Italian CUNA, but we are not going into that now.

Improved Breathing By New Cylinder Head

The BP has a new precision die-cast aluminum cylinder head. The head houses twin overhead camshafts driven by a single-stage cogged belt. The camshafts act on four valves per cylinder via inverted bucket-type tappets with wear-resistant clearance adjusting shims inserted atop the tappets, replacing the previous hydraulic lash adjusters. The mechanical tappet reduces frictional loss between the cam lobe and the tappet face, as well as reciprocating mass. It gives slightly more lift, 8.5 mm vs the previous 8.0 mm, and allows an optimized cam profile, which Mazda engine designers call, "functional cam profile." Optimized valve timing with increased overlap, together with the new cam profile, improves cylinder filling.

Valves are Vee-inclined at an included angle of 50 degrees in a compact pentroof-shaped combustion chamber. The intake valve diameter is 33 mm and the exhaust valve 28 mm.

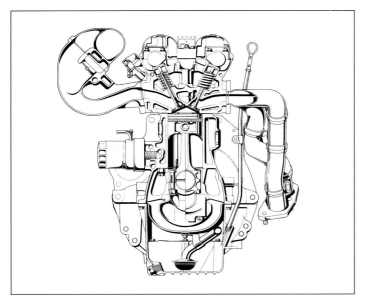

BP 1.8-liter engine is the updated version of the BP-ZE that powered the first-generation MX-5. The cylinder head is all new with a larger, more upright intake port design, mechanical inverted-bucket tappets with adjusting shims and optimized valve timing. The engine features a two-stage Variable Inertia Charge (induction) System (VICS).

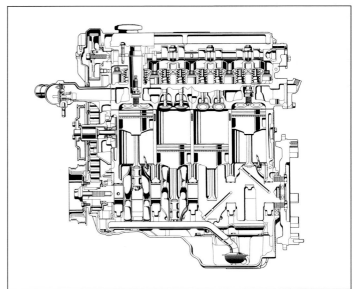

Longitudinal sectional view of the BP 1.8. The BP produces 140 bhp (138 bhp for California) SAE net at 6,500 rpm and 119 lb-ft (117 lb-ft for California) at 5,000 rpm on a 9.5:1 compression ratio.

A higher compression ratio of 9.5:1, a result of the raised-crown piston, without incurring weight increase, contributes to improved low- and mid-speed torque.

The intake port is now more upright, with its axis at 39.5

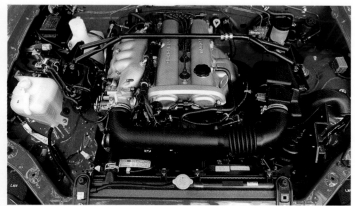
Type-BP 1.8-liter engine in the U.S. Sports model.

Exhaust manifold collects into single pipe. The TLEV exhaust system is equipped with a catalytic converter immediately downstream of the manifold, in addition to an underfloor catalyst.

Freer-flow 4-into-2 exhaust manifold replaces the 4-into-1 type for Europe and Japan.

degrees from the intake valve stem axis as compared with the previous version's 54 degrees. As a result of this redesign, the port's effective diameter has been increased from 37 mm to an equivalent of 39 mm, contributing to accelerated air flow, formation of tumble flow and improved combustion stability.

Fuel is injected sequentially to the individual cylinders by new compact, multi-point injectors which precisely aim spray to the intake valve openings.

Marked reductions in noise and vibrations were among the priority design and development targets. Mazda's advanced computer analysis and simulation programs were applied to the design of the cast iron cylinder block, which features contoured, weaved outer walls for added strength. The critical bearing support area within the block is heavily ribbed.

An intricately shaped steel VRSP (vibration reducing support plate) stiffens the open area at the bottom of the block and effectively reduces vibrations in the medium frequency zone. The BP engine's forged steel crankshaft is fully balanced with eight counterweights, and is supported by five main bearings. The flywheel has a lighter mass, contributing to about a 16-percent reduction in inertia resistance as compared with the earlier engine.

Variable Inertia Charge System

The induction system employs Mazda's Variable Inertia Charge System (VICS), which varies the effective intake tract length in order to obtain optimum cylinder filling by inertia charge effect. The U-shaped intake tract, whose curvature and varying diameters are optimized for efficient breathing, branches into two passages at the manifold's entry area. One of the passages is controlled by a butterfly shutter valve. This valve is closed by engine vacuum below 5,250 rpm, in effect, "lengthening" the tract to fully exploit the incoming air's ram effect. Above 5,250 rpm, the shutter valve is opened, "shortening" the tract to admit the required air volume for high power output.

The induction system incorporates a heated-wire mass air measurement device that ensures precise close-loop control with minimum resistance to the incoming air. The air-filter volume has been increased from the previous 4.6 liters to 6.0 liters to reduce induction noise, and the air-intake opening is now located immediately behind the headlamp cluster to introduce cooler air. The European version is fitted with triple resonators to minimize induction noise.

An aluminum radiator with plastic header and bottom tanks, along with an electric cooling fan, is standard on the MX-5. A large air intake in the facia results in a cooling efficiency gain of 6 percent versus the predecessor model. An additional electric fan is fitted when air conditioning is installed. The two fans turn in "counter-revolution" directions, directing cooling air onto the radiators more effectively.

Exhaust System — Emission Control and Sports Car Music

The distributorless ignition system is electronically controlled, and employs a piezo-electric knock sensor installed on the cylinder block as an input source.

A portion of the exhaust gas is recirculated into the combustion chambers to reduce pollutants, particularly oxides of nitrogen. EGR is electronically controlled by a 16-bit engine management computer, and is fed by an electric servo motor for precise metering (Japanese models don't have this.).

The engine management computer, which controls fuel injection, ignition and EGR, has five times the calculating capacity of the previous model. The system employs crankshaft angle and cam angle sensors, among its input sources, for precise control of engine functions.

The exhaust system differs according to the emission and noise regulations of the destination countries and regions. In the U.S. models, it is a 4-into-1 type, flowing into an under-floor monolith catalytic converter. The converter has a volume of 1.6 liters, and is housed in a round-sectioned, free-flow casting which occupies less space than the previous oval-sectioned one. The TLEV (transitional low emission vehicle) engine is equipped with a start-up catalyst of 1.0-liter volume, attached directly to the exhaust manifold, combined with an under-floor converter 1.0-liter capacity.

For other markets, the exhaust manifold is fabricated and welded with a stainless steel mounting base, and is 4-into-2, merging into dual tubes which collect into a single tube at mid-length to the under-floor 1.6 liter converter. The European model has a quick light-off converter.

Large-volume silencers, a 3.0-liter pre-silencer and a 17.5-liter main silencer are used in the MX-5 exhaust system. Mazda's engineers recognize that pleasant sounds are indispensable in a sports car. For the new MX-5, the sounds emanating from the engine and exhaust have been precisely analyzed at each frequency to eliminate irritating noise. They are proud that with this elaborate tuning, "sports car music" is successfully composed.

The Type B6 DOHC 16-Valve 1.6-liter

The B6 DOHC 4-cylinder engine is the latest, enhanced version of the B6-ZE which powered the original MX-5 Miata. In the first-generation series, it was replaced by the BP 1836-cc unit for the 1994 model year (July 1993). However, in certain European countries, the B6 1.6 continued to power an entry version, to receive a favorable "under 90-bhp" insurance classification as well as lower pricing.

The B6-powered series has now been re-introduced in Japan as well as in Europe. For the latter, its power output is increased to 81 kW EEC (110 bhp) at 6,500 rpm with maximum torque of 134 Nm (99 lb-ft) at 5,000 rpm on a 9.4:1

Type B6 1.6-liter unit for the European and Japanese entry models is an updated version of the original 1600, sharing the same improvements as the BP, except VICS.

compression ratio. Subjected to less stringent emission standards than Europe's Step II, the Japanese version is rated at 125 PS (metric horsepower) and 14.5 kg-m (105 lb-ft) at 5,000 rpm with the same compression ratio.

The B6 shares many of the larger unit's improvements, including mechanical tappets, knock sensor and electronically controlled EGR, but excluding the new cylinder head and VICS. The engine also continues with the ductile cast iron crankshaft.

DRIVETRAIN

The Type M15M-D 5-Speed Manual Transmission

The Mazda designed and manufactured type M15M-D 5-speed manual transmission served the naturally aspirated first- and second-generation RX-7s and the Miata. This transmission, already recognized as one of the world's top sports car gearboxes, has received numerous detail improvements for both the 1800 and 1600, except the Japanese 1800 series, which is equipped with a new 6-speed gearbox.

The clutch has a single dry plate with a diaphragm spring and a ball-throw bearing, and is hydraulically operated. The clutch plate's outer diameter is 215 mm for the BP 1.8-liter model and 200 mm for the B6 1.6-liter model. The lightweight clutch has less inertia effect, and its action is weighted and tuned for quick and positive engagement with a short pedal movement to assist quick gear shifts.

The gearbox is a two-shaft design with synchronizers on all gears. The first-gear synchronizer cone is a large 65 mm in diameter. A double-cone synchro is used on second gear for the BP 1.8-liter engine. The second-gear synchronizer cone for the B6 1.6-liter model also has a diameter of 65 mm. These improvements result in increased gearbox torque capacity.

The gears are shifted by a short, upright lever that moves with

instead of the previous three bands to optimize and smooth shift characteristics. The engine and transmission computers are interfaced, so that the former's torque output is momentarily reduced for smoother upshifts, both in automatic and manual shifting.

The automatic transmission for the U.S. adopts a conventional OD/OFF (overdrive cutoff) switch operated by a small button on the selector knob. For Japan, the transmission continues with Mazda's HOLD mode. The same button allows the driver to select and hold any of the lower three gears in this mode.

Gear ratios are: 1st, 2.450; 2nd, 1.450; 3rd, 1.000; 4th, 0.730 and Rev, 2.222, combined with a 4.100:1 final ratio for the BP 1.8-liter engine and a 4.300:1 ratio for the B6 1.6-liter.

New type-SB4A electronically controlled, 4-speed automatic transmission, also by Aisin, is available. The selector lever moves in a conventional, straight P-R-D-S-L gate. The U.S. model employs an OD/Off button, while the Japanese version continues with Mazda's HOLD mode that allows manual shifting and holding of lower gears.

Torsen limited-slip differential.

Final-Drive and Torsen Limited-Slip-Differential

The final-drive unit employs a lightweight 7-inch differential gear assembly. The front half of the housing is cast iron, while the aluminum rear half is integrally cast with a wide-span mounting bracket, which attaches the rear end of the power plant to the rear subframe.

A Torsen limited-slip differential is standard on the European 1.8-liter model and the Japanese 1800 series, and included in the U.S. Sports Package, all with manual transmission. The name is coined from "Torque sensing" and registered by Zexel-Gleason U.S.A.

The differential is unique in allowing the two primary functions of a limited-slip differential — torque management and differentiation — to occur simultaneously. In other words, it provides maximum tractive effort to each driving wheel, while allowing each driving wheel to respond to revolution differences dictated by vehicle direction and tire-to-road adhesion. It accomplishes these two tasks through the combination of its unique "Invex" gear design, the thrust forces generated by the Invex gearing and the frictional forces within the system.

During cornering, the Torsen differential enhances traction management because it possesses a built-in traction-control facility. Another inherent advantage is that it has a far superior "torque bias ratio." When a wheel-speed difference exists between the left and right driving wheels, the differential casing as a whole revolves at the left and right shafts' median speed. The frictional forces generated within the gear-washer-wall assembly exert a braking force on the faster spinning shaft and an accelerative force on the slower wheel. This means that more torque is directed to the slower-rotating wheel, whose tire is gripping the surface. During deceleration, the new B-type Torsen used in the MX-5 optimally distributes driving torque between the wheels. This is achieved by an increase in its coasting (throttle-off) torque bias ratio, which contributes to the car's stable transition between throttle-on and -off driving such as on a twisty road, enhancing the car's "turn-by-throttle" characteristics.

A single-piece, 60.5-mm-diameter, 1.8-mm-gauge, hollow propeller shaft with universal joints drives the final-drive unit. The drive shafts are of equal length and diameter, and incorporate double-offset joints at the inner ends and ball joints for the wheel attachments.

Power Plant Frame And Mounting

The Power Plant Frame (PPF) is an open-section, aluminum truss frame that connects the power unit and the final-drive/mounting bracket assembly, forming an integrated power plant. The PPF is tucked away under the car's floor pan, running on the right side of the propeller shaft.

It is press-formed from 6-mm-gauge aluminum sheet, and has

an intricate shape with varied section heights and widths (highest and widest: 163 mm and 60 mm, respectively) and a number of weight-saving holes. It weighs 10.8 lb (4.9 kg), including the attaching bolts, and measures 57.6 in. (1,463 mm) long.

The PPF greatly reduces drive-train bending during acceleration/deceleration resulting in a direct transmission of engine power to the driving wheels and improved driving feel.

The entire power plant is mounted at four points. The engine mounts are attached to the front subframe via brackets and semi-shear/compression mounts. The reinforced brackets (the right-hand one is now pressed steel instead of the previous cast iron) reduce the transmission of resonance, in effect, tuning engine sounds to be pleasant to the occupants' ears. The power plant's roll motion is arrested by a stopper block located under the engine.

The wide-span final-drive carrier bracket is attached to the rear subframe via two shear mounts. The aluminum bracket has two small notches on the backside of the rear arms. Should

the car be struck from the rear, the bracket breaks off, to prevent interference with the body/frame structure's "crumple zone" function, which absorbs impact energy.

Power unit and final drive are united by the Power Plant Frame.

MANUAL TRANSMISSION SPECIFICATIONS

Transmission		M15M -D	Y16M -D*
Type		Manual 5-speed	Manual 6-speed
Clutch		single dry plate, hydraulically operated	
Gearbox		All synchromesh	
Internal ratios	First	3.136	3.760
	Second	1.888	2.269
	Third	1.330	1.345
	Fourth	1.000	1.257
	Fifth	0.814	1.000
	Sixth	-	0.843
Final drive ratio			
BP 1.8		4.100:1	3.909:1
B6 1.6 Japan		4.300:1	n/a
B6 1.6 Europe		4.100:1	n/a
*Japanese BP 1.8-liter engine			

AUTOMATIC TRANSMISSION

Transmission		SB4A -EL
Type		Electronically controlled, 4-speed automatic with torque converter and planetary gearbox
Torque converter		with torque converter lockup cluch on 3rd and 4th
Internal ratios	First	2.450
	Second	1.450
	Third	1.000
	Fourth	0.730
Final drive ratio		
BP 1.8		4.100:1
BP 1.6 Japan		4.300:1

CHASSIS

The new MX-5 suspension adheres to Program Manager Takao Kijima's original concept for the MX-5: "Specific, classic and straightforward front and rear double-wishbones." Before taking charge of Mazda's sports car development programs, Kijima was chassis designer *extraordinaire*, and created such ingenious and dynamically superior sports car suspensions as the second-generation RX-7's DTSS (dynamically tracking suspension system) and the third-generation RX 7's DGCS (dynamic geometry control system). From his work with the RX-7, Kijima recognized the great potential of a double-wishbone suspension, and, indeed, the MX-5 fulfilled that promise, imparting joy to sports car enthusiasts all over the world.

Mazda's chassis designers and engineers, under the direction of Kijima, refined the MX-5 chassis, taking it to new heights in sports car dynamics.

The new MX-5's double-wishbone suspension has refined geometry and several important new components. Steering is by rack and pinion, again refined and improved in its precision. Power assisted steering is standard equipment on all models. All-wheel disc brakes provide stopping power. Two wheel/tire combinations are offered in the new MX-5 range.

Front Suspension

Double wishbones are formed by the pressed-steel upper A-arm and the pressed-steel, welded, box-sectioned, wide-base lower L-arm. The suspension-arm rubber bushings have steel collars between the outer and inner rubber rings, providing high lateral rigidity for precise handling, while ensuring sufficient fore- and-aft compliance for good ride quality.

The forged steel hub carrier/steering upright is among the lightest for the application, significantly reducing unsprung weight. The new-design upright, with revised attachment points for the tie rod, optimizes toe change on jounce. It adds 10 mm to the car's front track, with wheel-offset decreased from 45 mm to 40 mm in the model with the 1.8-liter engine and 195/50 tires. The front axle uses tapered roller bearings.

The suspension pickup points are carried by the front subframe, an intricately shaped, pressed-steel and welded structure that also supports the front of the power plant, as well as the steering gear. The subframe is rigidly bolted at eight points to the monocoque body shell. In addition, the subframe is reinforced by a pressed-steel brace bar. This redesigned member is now bolted to the frame at four points, contributing to the suspension's structural rigidity as well as body stiffness, which greatly reduces vibrations caused by road surface irregularities around the critical 110 km/h (69 mph) zone. The Japanese 1600 series is not fitted with the brace bar.

The concentric shock absorber and coil spring are attached via separate top mounts, which precludes interference caused by their reactive forces. The shock absorber functions more effectively at very low piston speeds. Benefits include: a reduced roll speed and increased yaw-rate, contributing to more agile turn-in; lower roll rate, resulting in reduced floating over large bumps and harshness; and more linear handling characteristics and a better ride.

The double-acting shock absorber is pressurized with inert gas, and it employs a new compact and more responsive bottom valve.

Additionally, the coil spring acts via a new rubber seat, which reduces transmission of road noise. Replacing the previous rubber bump-stopper is a new urethane design with superior compression and damping capacity, which increases suspension travel. It is more gradual and resilient in its action, reducing bounding on irregular surfaces during cornering at high lateral *G*s. It also has improved low-speed damping for a more linear response and improved ride quality.

A 22-mm-diameter solid stabilizer (anti-roll) bar is

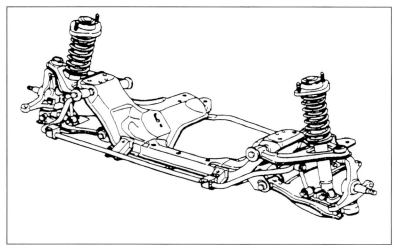

Double wishbone front suspension employs lower L-arms and upper A-arms, coil springs, tubular shock absorbers and an anti-roll bar.

Anti-roll bar now acts via ball-jointed links.

standard on the front suspension, acting on the lower A-arms via pivoted links newly connected by ball joints.

The front suspension's geometry has been refined with the lower arm's mounting brackets lowered by 5.7 mm. As a result, the front roll center has been lowered to 41 mm, while the rear roll center remains at 120 mm. The new roll-center height improves roll control without resorting to stiffer suspension settings which would be detrimental to ride quality. At maximum lateral acceleration, the ratio between inner and outer front-wheel lift has been optimized from 70:30 to 60:40. In addition, the lower front roll center contributes to reduced track change during jounce, resulting in better straight-line stability.

The new geometry enables the suspension to fully utilize its damping capability. Among its benefits are reduced transient roll and a more stable and controlled "diagonal" roll feel by virtue of an optimized relationship between the center of gravity and the roll axis.

Caster angle has been increased from the previous 4°26′ to 5°48′ and caster trail has been increased from 15 mm to 21.5 mm by moving the lower arm pickups slightly forward and the upper arm pickups rearward for improved straight-line stability regardless of road surface irregularities.

Front suspension travel is 93 mm in jounce and 82 mm in rebound.

Rear Suspension

The rear suspension's pressed-steel upper arm is a typical A-shape, while the lower arm looks more like the letter "H" with a wider hub-carrier mounting base, which ensures precise axle location. The lower arm is fabricated from pressed steel that is welded into a sturdy box-section that provides high lateral rigidity. The arm's lower surface has lightening holes to reduce unsprung mass. As in the front suspension, double, rubber-ring, steel-collar bushings are used on the subframe-side pivots.

The forged steel rear hub-carrier/upright is also a new design, adding 20 mm to the rear track with a 40-mm wheel offset instead of the previous 45 mm in the model with aluminum wheels. As in the front, concentric shock absorbers and coil springs with separate top mounts are fitted at the rear. This design eliminates interference between the reactive forces of the two components, enabling the shock absorber to function more effectively at very low piston speeds. The spring acts via a rubber seat, reducing transmission of road noise. The double-acting damper is pressurized with inert gas.

The rear suspension, like the front, is fitted with a new urethane bump-stopper providing more progressive movement and a linear spring/damping rate. Rear suspension travel has been increased by 10 mm in jounce to

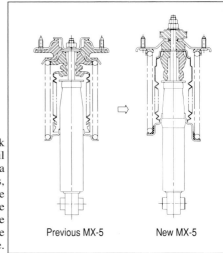

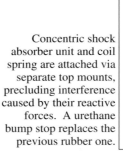

Concentric shock absorber unit and coil spring are attached via separate top mounts, precluding interference caused by their reactive forces. A urethane bump stop replaces the previous rubber one.

Previous MX-5   New MX-5

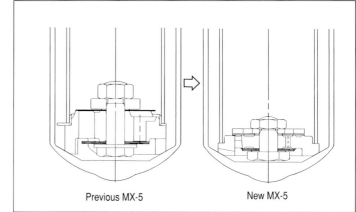

Previous MX-5   New MX-5

Shock absorber's bottom valve is compact and responsive.

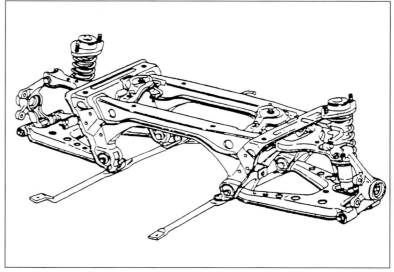

Rear suspension is also by double wishbones. As in the front, concentric shock absorbers and coil springs with separate top mounts are used, as is a progressive-rate bump-stopper.

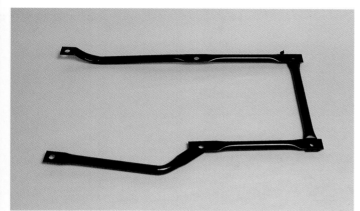

The rear subframe is reinforced by transverse and longitudinal brace bars.

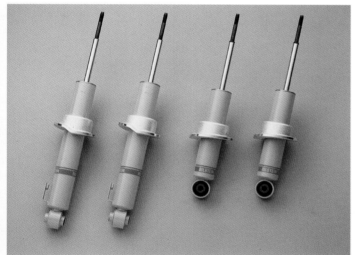

The U.S. Sports model and the Japanese RS are fitted with Bilstein shock absorbers.

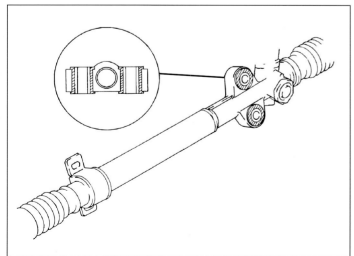

The steering's gear assembly is securely attached to the subframe cross-member via a new "eye-type" mount, instead of the previous U-clamp.

96 mm. Rebound travel is unchanged at 80 mm. The new urethane bump-stopper, like the one up front, increases the suspension's "virtual" travel, greatly improving ride, handling and roadholding.

The suspension's pickup points are attached to a fabricated steel welded subframe structure. This subframe also carries the final-drive unit which forms the rear portion of the drive train. The subframe is reinforced by an additional lateral and longitudinal brace bar assembly which, together with the front brace bar, reduces shaking and bouncing vibrations in the critical 110 km/h (60 mph) zone (the brace bar is not fitted in the Japanese 1600 series).

The rear suspension incorporates stabilizing toe-control geometry, which reacts to the lateral forces generated during maneuvers such as spirited cornering and rapid lane changes. The lower arm's wheel-side pivots, which carry the hub-carrier/upright, have rubber bushings of different elasticity rates. The rear pivot has a firmer rubber bushing than the front pivot. When subjected to lateral forces, the front bushing deforms more than the rear, resulting in a small amount of stabilizing wheel toe-in. An 11-mm diameter solid stabilizer (anti-roll) bar, attached on the lower arms via pivoted links, is standard at the rear.

Sports Package/1800RS Suspension

A Sports Package for the U.S. Miata and the Japanese Roadster RS1800 is equipped with a sports suspension consisting of firmer springs, Bilstein gas-filled shock absorbers with firmer damping characteristics, a thicker (12 mm vs 11 mm) rear anti-roll bar and Michelin Pilot SX GT 195/50VR15 tires on 15 x 6JJ aluminum alloy wheels.

Steering

The Mazda MX-5 is equipped with precise, power assisted rack-and-pinion steering. The steering has a quick ratio of 15:1 requiring just 2.6 turns of the steering wheel from lock-to-lock. The system's variable power assistance senses engine rpm.

The Japanese 1600 base model is fitted with manual steering.

The steering gear assembly is securely attached to the front suspension subframe cross member by a new "eye-type" mount. The eye is machined to fit the gear assembly, and is bolted to the subframe via rubber bushings with steel collars, in contrast to the previous U-clamp which "float-mounted" the gear assembly within rubber bushings. The new method provides more precise positioning of the steering gear assembly, and precludes variance in clamping tolerance, thus enhancing steering responsiveness.

A new four-spoke, 380-mm-diameter urethane steering wheel is standard. The rim is oval in cross section, resulting in a more comfortable grip. Together with improved packaging of the standard SRS airbag inflator within the center pad, the steering wheel has shed about 10 percent of its inertia moment, contributing to the steering system's responsiveness.

Available in the BP 1.8-liter model is a new stylish small diameter, three-spoke, leather-wrapped Nardi steering wheel. The center section neatly houses the standard SRS airbag. The wheel's moment of inertia has been reduced by about 30 percent compared to that of the previous model.

The steering shaft has been lengthened by 10 mm to provide additional impact absorbing capacity, and the column is reinforced to minimize transmission of vibrations at high vehicle speeds. Use of a stiffer rubber coupling for the intermediate shaft results in improved steering feel.

Brakes

Four-wheel disc brakes are standard on the MX-5. The front discs are 255 mm in diameter, 20 mm in thickness and are ventilated by internal finning. The solid rear discs are 251 mm in diameter and 9 mm thick. Calipers are a single-piston two-pin type. The front caliper is mounted aft of the wheel center line, and the rear caliper is mounted in front of the axle. The front pad area is 43 cm^2, and rear area is 26 cm^2.

An 8-inch vacuum servo assists braking. Dual hydraulic circuits are split front and rear. The rear circuit is pressure modulated by a proportioning valve to prevent premature locking of the rear wheels.

Four-sensor, three-channel ABS with a compact, lightweight hydraulic unit is available in the U.S. Miata, standard in the European MX-5 except the B6 1.6-liter base model, and standard in upper Japanese models in both the 1.8- and 1.6-liter series.

The parking brake is mechanically applied to the rear discs and incorporates an automatic adjustment mechanism.

Wheels and Tires

Standard wheel and tire combination is 185/60R14s on pressed steel, four-bolt, 14 x 6JJ wheels, except the Japanese base 1600 which is fitted with 14 x 5.5JJ wheels. The U.S. Sports Package and the Japanese 1800RS feature high-performance 195/50R15 tires on cast aluminum, five-spoke, four-bolt, 15 x 6JJ wheels. This combination is available on the European BP 1.8-liter model. Tires are a lightweight design, reducing mass by 0.6 kg per 15-inch tire and 0.5 kg per 14-inch tire.

Vented front disc is 255 mm in diameter and 20 mm thick. It is clamped by a single-piston two-pin caliper.

Solid rotor of 251-mm diameter and 9-mm thickness is used at the rear.

Michelin Pilot 195/50VR15 SX GT tires on 15 x 6JJ alloy wheels are the foot wear of the high-end 1800 series.

SUSPENSION SPECIFICATIONS

		NORMAL	SPORTS
FRONT SUSPENSION			
Type		independent by unequal-length pressed A-arms (double-wishbones), coil springs, telescopic shock absorbers and anti-roll bar	
Spring type		Coil	
spring rate kgf/mm		2.9	3.0
Shock absorber		Double-acting gas-filled	Bilstein double-acting, gas-filled
rate at 0.1 m/s rebound	kgf	62	58
jounce	kgf	35	23
rate at 0.3 m/s rebound	kgf	115	119
jounce	kgf	57	50
Anti-roll bar type		Solid torsion bar	
diameter		22*	22
Wheel travel (unladen) jounce	mm	93	
rebound	mm	82	
Geometry (unladen) camber	deg min.	0°6′	
caster	deg min.	5°48′	
king-pin inclination	deg. min.	11°38′	
toe-in	mm	3	
Front roll center	mm	41	
REAR SUSPENSION			
Type		independent by unequal length pressed (double-wishbones), coil springs, telescopic shock absorbers and anti-roll bar	
Spring type		Coil	
spring rate kgf/mm		2.1	2.21
Shock absorber		Double-acting, gas-filled	Bilstein double-acting, gas-filled
rate at 0.1 m/s rebound	kgf	62	63
jounce	kgf	35	26
rate at 0.3 m/s rebound	kgf	115	121
jounce	kgf	77	57
Anti-roll bar type		Solid torsion bar	
diameter		11	12
Wheel travel (unladen) jounce	mm	96	
rebound	mm	80	
Geometry (unladen) camber	deg. min.	-0°47′	
toe-in	mm	3	
Rear roll center	mm	120	

*Japanese B6 1.6-liter model has a 19-mm anti-roll bar

BODY AND EQUIPMENT

Improved Body Stiffness

The MX-5 body is of all-steel, welded unit-body construction with its main stress-carrying, longitudinal frame members running as straight as the layout permits. The low-slung sports car incorporates a large-section central tunnel straddling the power plant and deep-section side sills strengthened by extended inner reinforcements. The body's central section is thus like twin pontoons formed by the side sills and tunnel, greatly enhancing the body shell's rigidity. The junction of the tunnel with the lower dashboard is reinforced by large, heavy-gauge side gussets. Rear portions of the front longitudinal frames are attached to the central tunnel as well as to the dashboard. Likewise, the rear frames are connected to the tunnel as well as to the rear bulkhead.

Measures to improve the body's resistance to high amplitude vibrations, commonly referred to as "shake," include larger-, heavier-gauge reinforcement panels on the A-pillars, additional side sill gussets, plus larger-, heavier-gauge gussets to reinforce the tunnel's junction with the rear bulk head.

The body's torsional stiffness has been greatly enhanced, to an exceptional natural frequency of 17 Hertz. (One Hertz [Hz] equals one cycle of vibration per second.) Large, heavy components such as the power plant and suspension, tend to vibrate at frequencies of between 7 and 15 Hz. Raising the natural frequency of the body above this range is the most effective way to control noise and vibration.

Particular attention was paid to strengthening those parts of the body to which the suspension and suspension-carrying subframes are attached, thus providing the solid foundation essential to the car's outstanding dynamics. These measures reduce shaking forces at the bottom of the A-pillars by 35 percent, producing a significant improvement in dynamic rigidity. Structural stiffness of this area has been improved to the point that add-on braces are no longer required.

All-steel integral welded body shell of the new MX-5.

Crash Protection

Mazda's designers and engineers aimed at providing maximum occupant protection in case of an accident, surpassing stringent regulatory requirements, including the U.S. and Europe's side-collision tests. The company's advanced computer-aided structural analysis techniques were fully applied to the design of the new body, resulting in a strong central section and energy-absorbing deformable front and rear ends.

Measures taken to ensure the body's crash-worthiness and occupant protection include:
— Addition of an inner reinforcing member in each front longitudinal member
— A reinforced front cross member
— "Crash cans" on the front frame ends, which add 25 mm to their length, providing extra energy-absorbing capacity
— Allowing the suspension-carrying subframe to slide rearward on impact to absorb energy; side sills which overlap the doors to add strength
— A revised rear longitudinal frame structure, which deforms progressively on rear impact

The door is fitted with a combination of an inner reinforcement panel and a tubular impact bar at the beltline, as well as a mid-height, tubular impact bar. The hinge and latch areas are heavily reinforced. The overlap between the doors and side sills is enlarged to effectively absorb the impact energy in an accident.

In the trunk, a temporary spare tire is mounted in a rearward

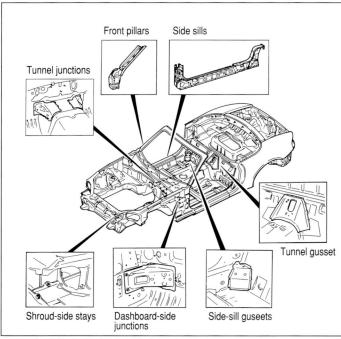

Body shell is strategically reinforced and strengthened.

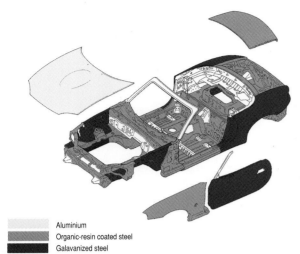

Aluminium
Organic-resin coated steel
Galavanized steel

Anti-corrosion measures employing organic-resin-coated steel and galvanized steel.

Each door incorporates twin impact bars.

Aluminum hood/bonnet is standard. It is about 8-percent larger than the previous model's, yet weight increase is minimal.

Front bumper inner reinforcement is made of "blow-mold" plastic. Bumper/facia is lightweight and resilient polypropylene. The reinforcement is attached to the body's front frames via "crash-cans."

tilted position. In the event of a rear-end collision, this layout absorbs the impact without directly transmitting crash forces to the front of the car.

The outer door handle is a new, larger, flush design facilitating easier pulling. High-tensile steel is used extensively in the construction of the body for strength and light weight. In addition, the aluminum hood/bonnet is about 8-percent larger than the previous model's, extending forward to the fixed headlamps. However, weight increases were minimized through the aid of computerized analysis and strenuous weight-saving efforts. The luggage compartment lid is made of thin-gauge steel sheet, again designed using Mazda's GNC computer program. The opening of the lid is assisted by a space- and weight-saving torsion bar spring.

Bumper System, Lighting and Rear-View Mirrors

The front and rear bumpers/facias are made of polypropylene plastic, painted/color-matched to the body. The front inner reinforcement bar is also made of plastic by a "blow-mold" process. This energy-absorbing light-weight bar is attached to the crash-cans. The rear reinforcement is a triple-box-section extruded aluminum bar. The front bumper system satisfies 5-mph (8 km/h) impact requirements, while the rear bumper meets the 2.5-mph (4 km/h) standard.

Compared with the previous MX-5's retractable front lighting system, the new MX-5 employs fixed, flush-mounted headlamp assemblies which contribute to a significant 5.6 kg weight reduction in this dynamically critical front overhang area. The lamp cluster includes a halogen headlamp and a directional signal indicator.

The tail lamp cluster is comprised of an integral tail/brake lamp and a directional signal indicator assembly housed under a refined, familiar oval lens. A rear high-intensity fog lamp is included in the cluster of the European model. A high-mount brake lamp is housed at the rear of the trunk lid.

Newly designed door-mounted mirrors feature integral top-casing rain gutters which deflect rain droplets away from the

The rear bumper reinforcement is a triple-box-section extruded aluminum bar. Rear bumper/facia is also made of polypropylene.

mirror's surface.

Soft Top

The ease of operation and weather protection provided by the original MX-5's manually folding soft top served as a benchmark for roadsters that followed. Mazda's engineers have successfully improved upon the design.

By far, the most significant change is the use of a glass rear window. This eliminates the scratching and ozone "fogging" which, over time, reduces rear outward vision through the original MX-5's plastic window. In addition, the top can now be stored/erected without unzipping/zipping the rear window, which was required with the previous design. The glass pane is imprinted with heated elements for demisting/defrosting. The glass window was incorporated without incurring weight penalty. In fact, the soft top's weight has been reduced by almost 1.3 kg, and its operating effort reduced significantly, making it the world's easiest roadster top to operate.

The soft top's weather sealing also has been improved, making it among the best in the segment for tight, no-leak protection. The redesigned soft top is also less prone to flapping.

Detachable Hardtop

A sheet molding compound (SMC) plastic hardtop is optional. In fact, the original hardtop fits the new MX-5, encouraging repeat customers who purchased this option. The top consists of a single-piece molding, enhancing its smooth contours and finish while achieving light weight. It also has a fixed glass rear window.

Wipers

On the driver's side, a "twisted" wiper arm is incorporated to avoid lifting during high-speed driving. Because of its finless design, it possesses excellent wiping performance even in a heavy rain and preserves forward vision.

SAFETY

Active Safety

Active safety means the driver must have total control of the car, and the car must respond to the driver's every command. The MX-5 Miata is an exceptionally responsive automobile with superb vehicle dynamics. Additionally, a good field of vision is another important safety factor.

Among the active safety measures incorporated in the MX-5, Mazda cites the following:
— Superior chassis dynamics.
— Outstanding accident/danger avoidance capability by the car's exacting handling. Optional ABS adds to this capability.

— Largest field of vision in the compact roadster class, a result of an expansive glass area, including the new glass rear window in the soft folding top, plus larger rear view mirrors incorporating rain-deflecting gutters.
— Driver environment with controls and instruments/gauges positioned for quick operation and viewing.

Passive Safety — Advanced Body Structure

Many of the measures taken to protect MX-5 occupants when an accident is unavoidable have been described in the Body section. Mazda conducted collision impact analysis using supercomputer technology and a series of actual crash tests. The body structure is the first line of occupant protection and includes:
— A strong passenger section to minimize deformation.
— Front and rear sections with controlled "crumple" zones to absorb impact energy.
— Reinforced pillars, stronger door hinges and latches.
— An impact-absorbing instrument panel.

Protective Occupant Environment

The interior is fully upholstered and includes soft-surface padding on all critical areas. The instrument panel extends rearward by 20 mm for added impact absorption, and includes knee-protecting panels. The A-pillar and door trim panels have energy-absorbing capabilities in the event of a side impact. The door also incorporates an inner pad to offer protection against impact.

Seat Belt System

Primary occupant restraints are the three-point, shoulder/lap safety belts. The belt system incorporates a direct-clamp mechanism. The European MX-5 is fitted with pre-tensioners, which automatically tighten the belts via a signal from a sensor and pyrotechnic tensioners.

Supplemental Restraint System (SRS) — Airbags

Dual SRS airbags are standard in the new MX-5. The airbag system performs a self-diagnostic check, and should a failure be detected, a warning lamp in the instrument cluster is illuminated.

SPECIFICATIONS AND PERFORMANCE DATA
(U.S.A. and European Models)

DIMENSIONS AND WEIGHT

External Dimensions

		U.S. Miata	European MX-5
Overall length	in. (mm)	155.3 (3,945)	156.5 (3,975)*
Overall width	in. (mm)	66.1 (1,680)	66.1 (1,680)
Overall height	in. (mm)	48.4 (1,230)	48.2 (12,25)
Wheelbase	in. (mm)	89.2 (2,265)	89.2 (2,265)
Track, front	in. (mm)**	55.7 (1,415)	55.7 (1,415)
rear	in. (mm)**	56.7 (1,440)	56.7 (1,440)
Ground clearance, unladen	in. (mm)	5.2 (130)	5.2 (130)

Interior Dimensions

Head room	in. (mm)	37.0 (942)	37.0 (942)
Leg room	in. (mm)	42.8 (1,086)	42.8 (1,086)
Shoulder room	in. (mm)	49.7 (1,263)	49.7 (1,263)
Luggage capacity	cu-ft (liters)	5.1 (144)	5.1 (144)
Curb Weight	lb (kg)		
U.S. model		2,299 (1,045)	n/a
European 1.8-liter		n/a	2,255 (1,025)
1.6 liter		n/a	2,233 (1,015
Weight distribution, front/rear, unladen		50/50	50/50

ENGINE

	U.S.	EUROPE	
	BP 1.8	BP 1.8	B6 1.6
Type	Inline 4-cylinder, water-cooled, DOHC, 4-valves per cylinder		
Bore x Stroke, mm	83.0 x 85.0	83.0 x 85.0	78.0 x 83.6
Total displacement, cc	1836	1836	1597
Compression ratio	9.5:1	9.5:1	9.4:1
Max power, bhp SAE @ rpm	140@6500	n/a	n/a
California, bhp SAE @ rpm	138@6500	n/a	n/a
EEC kW @ rpm	n/a	103@6500	81.6@6500
Max torque, lb-ft SAE net @ rpm	119@5500	n/a	n/a
California, lb-ft SAE @ rpm	118@5000	n/a	n/a
EEC Nm @ rpm	n/a	162@4500	134@5000
Fuel System	Multi-port electronic fuel injection		
Recommended Fuel	Regular grade unleaded gasoline		
Cylinder Block	Cast iron		
Cylinder Head	Die-cast aluminum		
Crankshaft	Forged steel	Forged steel	Ductile cast iron
Number of Main Bearings	5		
Camshaft Layout	Double overhead camshafts		
Camshaft Drive	Single stage cogged belt		
Number of valves per cylinder	4		
Valve Acting Mechanism	Direct-acting by mechanical bucket tappets		
Induction System	Variable inertia charge system		Individual tracts
Ignition System	Electronic; distributorless; piezo-electric knock-sensor		
Lubrication System	Force-feed by trochoid pump		
Oil Filter			
Lubricant Capacity, U.S. gal. (liters)	1.07 (4.0)	1.07 (4.0)	0.95 (3.6)
Cooling System	Water-cooled; aluminum radiator; electric fan		
Coolant capacity, U.S. gal. (liters)	1.53 (5.8)		

Fuel Tank Capacity, U.S. gal. (liters)		12.7 (50)		

DRIVE TRAIN

Manual Transmission		M15M-D		
Type		Hydraulically operated clutch; 5-speed manual gearbox; all synchromesh		
Gear Ratio	1st	3.136		
	2nd	1.888		
	3rd	1.330		
	4th	1.000		
	5th	0.814		
	Reverse	3.758		
Final Gear Ratio		4.100:1		
Automatic Transmission (U.S. only)		SB4-EL		
Type		Hydraulic torque converter with lockup clutch; planetary gear train, 4-speed automatic		
Gear Ratio	1st	2.450		
	2nd	1.450		
	3rd	1.000		
	4th	0.730		
	Reverse	2.220		
Final Gear Ratio		4.100:1		

CHASSIS

Front Suspension		Indendent by unequal length upper and lower arms (double-wishbones); coil springs; tubular shock absorbers; anti-roll bar		
Rear Suspension		Independent by unequal length upper and lower arms (double-wishbones); coil springs; tubular shock absorbers; anti-roll bar		
Steering		Rack-and-pinion; engine-speed-sensing variable power assistance		
Gear ratio		15:1		
Turns lock-to-lock		2.6		
Minimum turning circle, wall-to-wall ft.(m)		31.9 (9.7)		
Brakes				
Front		Ventilated discs; single-piston, two-pin calipers		
Rear		Solid ciscs; single-piston, two-pin calipers; vacuum serevo assisted		
Disc diameter, front	mm	255		
rear	mm	251		
Swept area, front	cm^2	43		
rear	cm^2	26		
Vacuum booster diameter	in.	8		
Parking brakes		Mechanical on rear discs		
Tires and Wheels				
Wheels		14 x 6JJ	14 x 6JJ	14 x 5.5JJ
Tires		185/60HR14	185/60HR14	185/60HR14
Optional wheels	***	15 x 6JJ	15 x 6JJ	n/a
tires		195/50VR15	195/50VR15	n/a
EPA Mileage Estimates				
Federal	mpg	25 city/29 high way	n/a	n/a
California	mpg	23 city/28 high way	n/a	n/a

Notes: * = with front license plate bracket

** = with aluminum wheels

*** = U.S. Sports Package; Europe optional on the BP 1.8-liter model

Chapter

2

DEVELOPMENT STORY

SPORTS CAR ECSTASY

Soichiro Honda changed his mind overnight, not an unusual trait for the genius engineer-entrepreneur. Honda Motor Company, by then the world's biggest motor cycle producer and a fledgling automobile manufacturer, purchased a large piece of land in the city of Suzuka, Japan, in the late Fifties with the intention of building a factory. Management deemed the site too big for the projected plant, so they decided to turn part of it into an athletic facility for Honda's diligent employees. Then, Mr. Honda decreed that he wanted a proper race track, the first of its kind in Japan.

The Suzuka Circuit was thus built, and the Japanese were treated to the sight of racing cars of various shapes, sizes and nationalities competing on the new race track. Suddenly, the car-producing members of the Japanese auto industry were deeply involved in racing, in win-or-bust frenzies that lasted a couple of years in the early Sixties, until the self-imposed constraint against advertising racing victories took effect.

Hiroshi Yamamoto, combustion research engineer by education and training, joined Mazda, then Toyo Kogyo Company, in 1962. A year later, Mazda plunged into racing with the tiny R360 coupe, powered by a light alloy (magnesium was liberally used), air-cooled, overhead-valve V-twin engine mounted in its hind end. The car was no match for those furious, smoke-belching two-stroke Suzukis and Subarus in the under-400-cc class in the first Japanese Grand Prix. For the 1964 race, Mazda prepared a fleet of the brand new Carol, another petite rear-engine sedan powered by an aluminum water-cooled, OHV, inline 4-cylinder engine, displacing all of 360 cc! Yamamoto was a member of the newly formed Mazda competition department. The team was to taste another ignominious defeat in the 1964 race.

The Hiroshima-based manufacturer was undaunted, and its assaults on the world's race tracks would continue for the following four decades, with its various performance models, both with the reciprocating piston- and rotary-engines, culminating in the outright win in the 1991 Le Mans 24-hour Endurance Race for Sports Cars with its quad-rotor 787B car. Fifteen years of Yamamoto's engineering career were devoted to Mazda's competition activities, including early Le Mans efforts.

The deputy director of the office of product program managers says, "Motor sports and sports cars must be in our veins." Reminded that Mazda is one of only a few automakers who are volume producers of two sports cars (the Miata and the RX-7, the latter still offered in Japan) in its lineup, apart from such specialists as Porsche, Yamamoto grins and corrects, "No, we had three at one time. Remember the mid-engine, gull-wing micro-sports AZ-1?"

After his long racing sojourn, Yamamoto returned to the Hiroshima engineering center's mainstream activities, soon to become a chief engineer responsible for evaluation and development of new vehicles. He was then appointed program manager for the company's ultimate high-performance Cosmo luxury car, powered by an extraordinary twin-turbo, 3-rotor engine. The Cosmo development progressed side-by-side with the three ongoing sports car projects.

CORPORATE AGONY

This economic battleship group called Japan was once thought to be unsinkable, but of late it has developed nasty leaks. The individual members of the Japanese automobile industry have taken arms against the turbulent sea of troubles as best they could, with varying degrees of successes and failures. Among them, Mazda has had more than its fair share of problems. It was hardest hit by the Great Oil Crunch in the 1970s, and appeared, for a while, to be falling into an abyss.

Miraculously, the Hiroshima company pulled out of a massive stall, helped by an infusion of yen from its main bankers and a hefty dollar order from its American partner Ford for the Courier compact pickup based on Mazda's B-series truck. According to some sources, it was a banker-executive sent over to help Mazda recuperate, who encouraged the development of a brand new sports car, the first-generation RX-7. The RX-7 provided some much needed cash flow to the company's pinched financial coffers.

In the early Eighties, Mazda was given a clean bill of health, and once again was on the path to a promising yonder. Its course steadied by its mainstream models, Mazda sought to expand its product lineups, conceiving and developing "off-line" projects, which bred successful models as the MPV, the MX-5 and the revived "Kei" (light in Japanese) car Carol.

Not content, Mazda embarked on an even more ambitious and grandiose expansion strategy, expanding its Japanese dealer networks with no less than five brand names versus much larger Ford's three nameplates. Mazda also began a premium car line called Amati in America, pursuing a course previously set by Honda, Toyota and Nissan with their Acura, Lexus and Infiniti divisions, respectively. The Amati luxury lineup was also to include a V12-powered luxury sedan.

This "expansionism" could not have come at a worse time. Out of the blue, Japan's "Bubble Economy" popped, blowing Mazda into another bad spin. Contraction began in earnest. First, the Amati project was aborted. But the Hiroshima company was also in dire need of another infusion of operating capital, which was provided by Ford whose stake in the company has since increased to a majority (the biggest among stock-holders) 33.4-percent. Together with the financial involvement, Dearborn sent in a team of top executives, including two consecutive presidents, to help Mazda regain its stability.

Sports and performance cars can be vulnerable in such stormy weather; they are "wants" not "needs." Mazda's largest and smallest, the exotic Cosmo and the AZ-1, suffered a quick demise. In addition, spiraling insurance premiums and the rising power of the yen forced the Japanese to pull out of the mainstream sports car arena in the U.S. and Europe. Nissan stopped exporting the 300ZX, and Toyota the MR-2, which were subsequently discontinued in Japan, and Mazda the RX-7 (which is still offered in Japan).

The program for the MX-5 replacement got under way in the spring of 1994, when Mazda's state of financial affairs were at rock bottom. How did the new Ford management team feel about the MX-5 Miata and Mazda's plan for a second-generation model? Tadahiko Takiguchi, Mazda veteran and senior managing director in charge of product development, relates, "Not a murmur of dissent was heard from the board members — the new expat executives and my own country-men-colleagues alike — on the MX-5 issue. On the contrary, we received hearty encouragement from all quarters." The MX-5 had been paying handsomely to the company's coffers, and its replacement was to proceed on course and on schedule.

Actually, Hiroshi Yamamoto had assured some key members of the Roadster (the Miata's Japanese name) Club of Japan on more than one occasion that he would preserve the original

car's exterior through the remainder of this century, meaning no major change would be carried out. However, more Draconian crashworthiness requirements that he thought would not take effect until the year 2000 were being implemented. To meet 1998 side-impact requirements, the body's inner structure would have to be drastically altered, which would entail changing its outer appearance. In the meantime, computer technology had been making quantum leaps, enabling faster and more weight-, performance- and cost-efficient design and development processes. So it was time to do a new car.

THE SPORTS CAR TEAM

Takao Kijima's strength and favorite domain since joining Mazda in 1967 had always been in chassis design. Starting out on early light car chassis, he designed many interesting and highly effective suspension systems, which included the 323, the second- and third-generation RX-7, the first-generation Miata and the grand touring Cosmo, as well as the analysis and refinement of the Le Mans-winning 787B race car. During the pre-Bubble-burst period, Mazda adopted a three-vehicle-center strategy in order to rapidly expand its product line. For logistical convenience, if nothing else, the sports car group found a strange home, in the Center No. 3 which was responsible for commercial vehicles. Kijima's talent was

At one time, Mazda had three sports car and a super grand touring car projects and a serious racing program occurring simultaneously.

Hiroshi Yamamoto, deputy director — the office of product program managers.

The first-generation MX-5.

The RX-7 rotary-powered sports car is still offered in Japan.

The AZ1 mid-engine, gull-wing micro sports car.

The Cosmo Super Grand Touring car powered by a triple-rotor, sequential-turbo rotary engine. Hiroshi Yamamoto took personal charge of this extraordinary car project as program manager.

Mazda took on the world in sports car racing: the 1991 Le Mans 24-hour endurance race winner, the 787B.

promptly called upon to design the suspension of the new Titan workhorse truck. He prides himself on having created one of the best handling cargo haulers in the business!

After the Bubble Burst, another reorganization took place, consolidating all product engineering activities under the office of program managers. Of the original sports car leader trio, Hiroshi Yamamoto became the deputy director of the office. Takaharu "Koby" Kobayakawa, program manager for the RX-7 and *de facto* racing director who led Mazda's Le Mans challenge to victory, took over the helm of the company's Design (styling) department, which had been dealt a severe jolt in the aftermath of the Bubble Burst. Koby was to oversee all of the new Miata's styling, from the inception of the new shape through its design-release phase.

Takao Kijima was now to form his own sports car team as the program manager for sports cars (note plurals), and to proceed with the design and development of the new roadster sports car. His team was a formidable one.

Takashi Takeshita, veteran sports car tuner who had worked on the original Miata and the third-generation RX-7 with then-chassis-designer Kijima, was the assistant program manager in charge of evaluation and testing, Mazda's way of describing development. Nobuyuki Nakanishi, a power train designer, was placed in charge of engineering design.

Koichi Hayashi of the Hiroshima design center was appointed assistant program manager for styling design, or, more plainly, chief stylist of the new sports car. Munenori Yamaguchi was Kijima's lieutenant and would see the program proceed to its fruition.

One could safety declare that it was the original Miata that brought about the renaissance of the compact, affordable open-bodied sports car. Kijima would say, yes, Mazda welcomed newcomers from the renowned European marques, embracing them all as friendly competitors, to expand the revitalized market segment. But, was Mazda's sports car team concerned about these new competitors? "To say no is immodest," admits development chief Takeshita. "We were concerned. So much so that Yamamoto, Kijima and our team made a number of midnight runs, driving our collection of latest open sports cars

on twisty mountain roads about 60 miles outside Hiroshima." The team reached a unanimous conclusion: the toughest competitor in terms of the sheer joy of driving a lightweight sports car, was their own, the first-generation Miata!

As Kijima asserts, the Miata's spirit is perpetual, and would require no conceptual revision. It would continue to be a lightweight, compact, front-engine, rear-wheel-drive, open-bodied sports car. Kijima's guiding caution to his team was:

$$I = I_0 + mr^2$$

in which **I** represents yaw (polar) inertia moment; **m** mass and **r** distance from the center of gravity. He explained that 1-kg located at the nose, 40.0 inches from the center of gravity, equals 100 kg at 4.0 inches away from the center of gravity. So concentrate mass within the wheelbase as close to the CG as possible, and lighten the whole car, part by part.

Ronald J. Leicht, Mazda's astute marketing honcho, received some nudges from the field, both in Japan and the U.S., for a bigger Miata replacement. The plea, more vocal, also reached Yamamoto and Kijima from the American shore, where it was hoped a larger car would fill, at least partially, the vacuum left by the RX-7's lamented departure.

This was one concession they would adamantly oppose. They had seen the RX-7, originally conceived as a sports car combining breathtaking rotary-performance with an affordable price tag, grow in size, sophistication and price, taking it out of the lightweight arena (Ironically, the RX-7's upscaling resulted in the creation of the MX-5, so the corporate coin had the proverbial two sides). Ron Leicht did not press the size issue. He is a sports car enthusiast who has owned a number of high-performance automobiles, including a Cobra and a DeTomaso. He knew it was best to leave the program in the capable hands of Mazda's sports car team.

Takao Kijima, program manager for both the new MX-5 and the RX-7.

Kijima's gospel truth: "A 1-kg mass carried at the extreme end of the overhang is equal to a 100-kg weight near the vehicle's center of gravity. Therefore, the vehicle's mass must be placed within the wheelbase, as close as possible to the CG.

1kg　1900mm　190mm　100kg

1kg　100kg　CG

1900mm　190mm

DESIGN

A car approaches from a hundred yards away. At a glance, you think it looks like an MX-5 Miata. As the car closes within 50 yards, you are happy to see that it is a Miata.
As it flashes by, yes, it's a Miata, and it's the new Miata! That's the kind of a car the new MX-5 is.
— *Tom Matano*

Miata Physique

Koichi Hayashi, assistant program manager — Design for sports cars, was asked by an auto writer who specializes in styling to describe the design concept of the new MX-5 Miata. He answered, "No conceptual revision whatsoever. Our entire MX-5 team cherished the original Miata's inborn soul, which is perpetual, not a mere concept, And we believe the new car has *'Physique'* rather than *'Exterior'* and *'Interior:'* Physique is the structure, strength and form of the whole car."

Tsutomu Tom Matano, executive designer of Mazda's Irvine, California, R&D center, echoes this precise sentiment, "We like to think of it as a Miata that has been working out at the gym, adding muscle and tone." It is Miata through and through.

When Takaharu Kobayakawa took over Mazda's design activities in the summer of 1994, the search for the new MX-5 design theme had already begun at the company's four design centers: the Hiroshima center where Hayashi took charge of the new car design project, the advance studio in Yokohama near Tokyo, Tom Matano's Mazda R&D studio, in Irvine, California and the European center near Frankfurt, Germany.

Each studio created its own theme proposal in the forms of sketches followed by scale models. And each theme had its own distinctive cultural, automotive and artistic interpretation of the region and design people. However, they all honored one unwavering discipline issued by program manager Takao

Takaharu "Koby" Kobayakawa was in charge of Mazda's Styling Division from the beginning to the end of the new Miata design activities.

Kijima: Each design must adopt the MX-5's unified power plant configuration with the engine placed "front-midship" driving the rear wheels. In addition, the outer dimensions had to be true to the LWS principle (lightweight sports car) achieving light weight and optimum weight distribution for outstanding dynamics. No mid-engine, or front-wheel-drive alternative would be considered this time around.

Hayashi confesses that inwardly he did not want to be in charge of the new design, for he was a key member of the Irvine design team which had created the original car. How could he ever dream of changing his eternal love? A happy torment, really. The first thing he did was to look at the original Miata, and jot down the key ingredients of the car that aroused such strong emotions: sensuous styling; original expression; simple, smooth surface treatment; plenty of room for customizing; and above all, the support of passionate, enthusiastic Miata owners.

Hayashi's course was clear: succession and development of the original Miata concept. The more contemporary exterior design theme his team developed included round headlamps evocative of the original Cosmo 2-seat coupe and latter-model air-cooled 911, strong blisters on the fenders conveying a more robust looks.

The Yokohama studio retained pop-up headlamps in its theme sketch. However, covers were not quite flush to the body, to impart a lithe and modern countenance, combined with a smoothly contoured body.

Mazda R&D of Europe's (MRE) sketch showed a more voluminous and aggressive roadster with a raised beltline, a lowered windshield and some interesting and modern Teutonic cues.

Tom Matano's strength was his "black" crystal ball, which showed things more clearly, especially sports car and Miata things, under the blazing southern California sun. For the benefit of the other studios, which might not have as much "seer power" as Irvine, Matano prepared a couple of cartoon illustrations to deliver Mazda R&D America's (MRA) conviction and perspective. One of them showed the four key ingredients of the original Miata: Inspired sensation; Affordable; Fun; and Symphony with Nature. "These become 'Givens' for the next generation. We will have to make the same kind of impact as the first one did!," delivers 'Professor Matano,' donning a scholarly hat, white garb and grayer (and quite a bit less) hair than his chief designer. The car's side-view theme is straight and neither a wedge (low nose, high rear deck) nor an "anti-wedge (high nose, low deck).

In the mind of MRA designers, the new Miata was going to be a natural evolution of the original theme. So they put the Miata on a work-out program. Speaking on the car's behalf, the cartoon professor translates, "I started jogging in '89 when I was round and cute. In the subsequent 10 years, I built up more muscle." On the specifics, the professor reflects: "The straight, plane rocker panels and door cuts of the current (original) car lack interest. Therefore, more emphasis should be placed on the rocker area for the next generation."

MRA did its homework well, not only on paper but in the field, with a number of concept vehicles reflecting the direction their next-generation Miata would take and laying the groundwork for their forthcoming challenge. These are the M Speedster, M Coupe and the Trunk Car, which are illustrated in Chapter 4.

Three Candidates In Full-size Models

To the delight of program manager Kijima and the team, every one of the four centers' theme sketches expressed the soul of the MX-5, differing only in detail design cues reflecting their specific cultures and regions. However, a choice had to be made. Three theme sketch proposals, one each from Hiroshima, Yokohama and Irvine, were chosen to be converted into full-size models at their respective studios, with a completion date of January, 1995.

Merits and weaknesses of each design were carefully

Theme Search

Hiroshima's concept of the MX-5 Miata.

Mazda's four design centers, in Japan, Europe and the U.S.A., searched for the design theme. This modern proposal was from the Hiroshima Design Center (known among the insiders as MC — short for Mazda Corporation).

Early theme sketches.

The Yokohama, Japan studio (MRY) continued with the pop-up headlight theme.

Mazda's European center near Frankfurt (MRE) sends in this voluminous design.

The California studio's (MRA) thoroughly-Miata approach. These '94 sketches by Ken Seward led to the final design.

evaluated, and the Hiroshima and Irvine themes were selected, called "Theme A" and "Theme B," respectively. Refinement of the designs progressed at a fast pace in Hiroshima and Irvine through the summer of 1995, beginning with the first and second full-size clay models and evolving to the life-like plastic mockups.

The Hiroshima model still featured fixed round headlamps, but the first clay model's matching taller taillamps had been replaced by an evolutionary version of the original Miata rear lights. An upswept accent line, running from the front fender, through the door and continuing to the rear wheel opening, gave the profile a more masculine feel. The Hiroshima designers created a subtle "lip" around the lower door cutout on the rocker panel to add depth to the design. In addition, the lower, rear portion of the door rose up in a curve, quite like Tom Matano's concept Miatas. Actually, this was an important functional element: the enlarged area aft of the door allowed for substantial reinforcement of the body structure, essential to the forthcoming side-impact protection regulations in the Miata's three major markets, the U.S., Europe and Japan.

Matano's team jealously guarded the original Miata's spirit. Auxiliary lamps were integrated within the flush headlamps, making them the "eyes" of the Miata. Its mouth, still retaining a hint of the original car's adolescence, was set in a strong jaw (the sculptured facia/bumper). More emphasis was evident in the sculptured rocker panel. Also, a strong visual element appeared on the lower quarter panel, continuing onto the rear facia/bumper's side, and reappearing on the bumper's rear face.

The Irvine center's design was finally selected for the new Miata. Chief designer Hayashi says, "It was not a case of one team winning, and others losing. The design was chosen to the

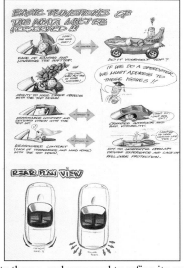

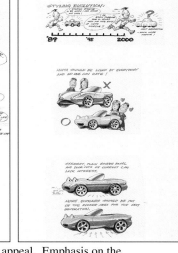

California cherished the original Miata theme, and proposed to refine its appeal. Emphasis on the rocker panel is obvious.

Early studies by clay models (January 1995).
Hiroshima, Yokohama and Irvine, California, pursued the theme search via clay models of their respective proposals.

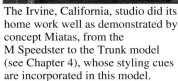

Yokohama full-size clay model. Door pulls are carry-over.

The Irvine, California, studio did its home work well as demonstrated by concept Miatas, from the M Speedster to the Trunk model (see Chapter 4), whose styling cues are incorporated in this model.

Hiroshima's modern roadster sports car theme with round headlamps. Door shape is similar to the first-generation Miata.

hearty endorsement of all involved in the new Miata design and development. After the selection, the final design was brought to Hiroshima for further refinement, engineering and production with passionate support from all the centers."

"There is neither East nor West, Border, nor Breed, nor Birth, When two strong men stand face to face, though they come from the ends of the earth!," observes the English writer Rudyard Kipling.

The twain met, and they worked face-to-face, hand-in-hand for their common goal: the new MX-5 Miata.

Give Us 1.5 Millimeters On Each Fender!

Kijima's object was seemingly immobile. Yet, Koichi Hayashi felt an irresistible urge. "The car's widest point in its cross section had been moved higher, to add more emphasis and accent to the fenders' volume." Hayashi says, "The strong shoulder created a negative impression that the wheels were tucked in. Our esthetic desire and the engineers' dynamic objective met, and the tracks were widened, 10 mm at the front and 20 mm at the rear, pushing the wheels outward. Still, we wanted more metal on the fenders to balance the car's visual balance."

When Hayashi presented his request for a 3-mm (all of 0.12 in.) increase in the car's width during an engineering meeting, lightning struck. He was branded a villain, a traitor and worse. But Hayashi persisted, and finally won his precious millimeters, which, in the end, grew to a generous 5 mm in the overall width of the car.

Hiroshima's Theme "A" and California's Theme "B" model development (August 1995).
Hiroshima and California refined their respective models through scale- and full-size models. The former's round-headlight model, is now called "Theme A," and the latter's "Theme B." The Yokohama proposal is no longer in competition.

This is Hiroshima's first full-size model of Theme A. The door shape is similar to MRA's.

Refinement of the first Theme A model is suggested.

Refined first Theme A model.

Designers and modellers at work in the Irvine, California, studio.

California's design is "Theme B." This is the second full-size clay model.

Final Theme A plastic mockup.

MRA-fabricated Theme B plastic mockup. Note the door pull is still carry-over.

The search for the interior design theme progressed in a manner similar to the exterior, with the four centers submitting their proposals in sketches. Hiroshima imposed two conditions: The design must incorporate Mazda's traditional "T-shape" sports car instrument panel and round vent outlets, hallmarks of the original Miata. And like the exterior, Hayashi wanted an integrated, youth-oriented interior without the mildly "ToysЯUs" built-up look of the original Miata. (The U.S. first-generation Miata received a redesigned instrument panel, with passenger-side SRS airbag installation, halfway in its life, but the right-hand-drive version kept the original IP throughout.)

Two candidates emerged from the original proposals: a more horizontal theme with a full-width instrument panel hood, and a more distinctive proper "T" panel with integrated IP and center console, in which four eye-ball vents were topped by strong "brows." The latter was selected as the new car's design theme.

The Italian specialist Nardi provides a leather-wrapped, three-spoke steering wheel on upper models. For Nardi, it was an-SRS-airbag-or-bust situation, confides Laura Blossfeld, an independent designer from Germany who worked on the Nardi design. The Mazda wheel was among the first that successfully incorporated SRS while retaining the design's light-weight, sporty appearance.

Storage space, or lack of it, was a target of criticism in the original Miata. The design and engineering teams, many of whom owned Miatas, tackled this major source of owner dissatisfaction. The glove compartment was enlarged, and each door now contains a map pocket molded into the gas-injection-formed trim panel. Another pocket is provided on the passenger side seatback, and there's also a mesh pocket in the optional Wind Blocker.

It was a cold December day in 1985 when Koby Kobayakawa, senior product evaluation engineer at the time, decided to take the 323 convertible prototype, along with its European competitors, to a ski resort with its top down! He insisted, "What is a car worth, if it cannot be driven all year round?" His hapless engineers were chilled to the bone, and Koby, man of forged steel, was no exception. They knew it was backdraft that was chilling them, so why not block it. A hastily devised curtain

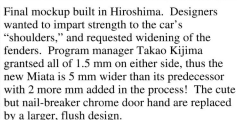

Final mockup built in Hiroshima. Designers wanted to impart strength to the car's "shoulders," and requested widening of the fenders. Program manager Takao Kijima grantsed all of 1.5 mm on either side, thus the new Miata is 5 mm wider than its predecessor with 2 more mm added in the process! The cute but nail-breaker chrome door hand are replaced by a larger, flush design.

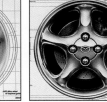

Standard 14-inch wheel design.

15-inch painted alloy wheel design.

15-inch chrome-plated wheel design. All wheels have five-spokes.

After-the-fact sketches showing the design continuity between the new and incumbent, and highlighting the new car's refinement.

was placed behind the rear seat, and *voilà,* the heater was directing warm air into the foot and lower torso area. Koby named it "Aero Curtain," which was promptly installed in the production Familia Cabriolet for Japan.

When Koby took over the second-generation RX-7, his first project was the convertible. It was fitted with the "Wind Blocker" board (still called "Aero Board" in Japan). Takao Kijima was Koby's sidekick in the design and development of the second- and third-generation RX-7s.

Kijima knew he had to have the Wind Blocker. He wanted the new Miata to be a year-round open sports car, even though it would be fitted with a soft top that would fit tighter than ever.

As in the exterior design theme search, the four centers submitted their interior proposals. Common among them was the use of round vent outlets on the instrument panel, one condition imposed by Hiroshima as an important Miata design cue.

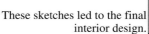 These sketches led to the final interior design.

Italian specialist Nardi adapted an SRS airbag installation to its 3-spoke design for the MX-5.

These are idea sketches for the Japanese 1800 with the speedometer and tachometer needles resting at the six o'clock position. Japanese cars are all governed to a maximum speed under 180 km/h.

Study of seat shapes, stitch patterns and colors based on the basic framework.

Final seating buck with the standard 4-spoke steering wheel.

Chief designer Koichi Hayashi (behind the wheel) checks the final seating buck.

MIATA'S HEART — THE ENGINE

Straight-forward, Twin-Cam, Four-Banger

"Straight-forward, naturally-aspirated, double-overhead-camshaft, 4-cylinder engine, burning regular-grade unleaded fuel," declares Hiroshi Yamamoto, deputy director — the office of program managers. "No turbocharger, no supercharger, and no variable valve timing device," he asserts.

Mazda has no aversion to such power boosting and torque lifting technology. On the contrary, Mazda held a very unique position, having three world's "firsts" in power train technology in series production: the rotary engine, the Comprex pressure-wave supercharger on a passenger-car diesel, and the Miller-cycle principle and Lysholm positive-displacement compressor combination for a high-power, high-efficiency V6. The Comprex diesel has recently been replaced by a less complex (no pun intended) and more fuel-efficient turbocharged, direct-injection diesel in the new, compact 626 for Europe. The other two firsts are very much alive today, powering the RX-7 and the Millennia S. And it's an open secret that Mazda is evaluating a Lysholm-supercharged 4-cylinder engine.

As for turbocharging, a big IHI instrument pumped up the output of the type-BP twin-cam 1836-cc engine (the same unit that powers the Miata) to close to 190 bhp in the all-wheel-drive 323 GT-R hatchback of circa 1991. And there was more on the tap, the limiting factor being the torque capacity of the existing side-winder gearbox.

In addition, the recently updated Familia (Protegé in the U.S.) series for Japan has a revamped 1.5-liter engine fitted with a continuously variable intake valve timing system.

So why such obstinate insistence on a straight-forward four-banger, especially when higher power and a wide spread of usable torque were among the power train's priority objectives? Program manger Kijima responds, "Because we wanted a direct, 'engine-attached-to-the-toes' responsiveness. Development chief Takashi Takeshita adds, "Reverberating response to your command."

It is not uncommon for 1.8-liter sports engines in recent Japanese sporty cars to put out 150 to 170 bhp. Honda's naturally aspirated, VTEC-equipped, DOHC 1.8 in the Integra R attained a magic 100-bhp-per-liter of displacement. Mazda's engine designers and development engineers were not out to challenge absolute numbers. Rather, they wanted to endow the type-BP inline-4 with a willingness to rev smoothly and a good spread of low- and mid-range torque, combined with high-speed power in the order of around 140 bhp, which is about the norm for its recent 1.8-liter European competitors.

Breath Freely

A new cylinder head was cast for the mainstream BP engine to improve breathing and combustion. The intake port is more upright, with its axis at 39.5 degrees from the intake-valve stem axis as compared with the previous version's 54 degrees. The port diameter also has been increased from 37 mm to 39 mm, and the wall where two ports merge into one has a sharper edge. These changes accelerate charge flow into the combustion chamber by as much as 10 percent, generating tumble flow which improves combustion. The intake port height is a critical factor, so an elaborate casting method was devised, incorporating a small protrusion in the port's lower wall and thus ensuring the precise positioning of the mold, controlling the height.

The use of a mechanical tappet, an inverted bucket type with a clearance adjusting shim, instead of the previous hydraulic lash adjuster, saves 200 grams, exerts 25-percent less load on valve springs and reduces mechanical friction. It also allowed Mazda designers to arrive at a more radical cam profile, which they called "Multi-Function" profile, "function" in this case referring to mathematical quantity. In the valve-timing diagram, the Multi-Function profile is shaped more like a trapezoid with the top flat section representing the valve's full opening duration, versus a conventional profile's hump shape with a shorter duration. The MF profile also increases valve lift, from the previous 8.0 mm to 8.5 mm. Valve timing also has been optimized for efficient filling and scavenging of the cylinders.

In the early development of the BP engine, the designers attempted to obtain optimum performance, combining low- and mid-speed torque with high-end power using a fixed-length intake manifold. They tried various configurations, tract sizes and lengths. More torque is obtained with longer tracts, but the computer simulation showed that because of a decrease in charge pulsation, high-speed power wouldn't be produced. This was really a trial-and-error process, which entailed burning a lot of midnight oil testing numerous tract shapes and sizes.

Finally, they decided they needed one variable — Variable Inertia Charge System, VICS — for short, with which Mazda has had a wealth of experience.

Each U-shaped intake tract, whose curvature and varying diameters are optimized for efficient breathing, branches into two passages at the manifold's entry area, one passage being controlled by a butterfly shutter valve. The valve is closed by engine vacuum below 5,250 rpm, in effect lengthening the primary intake tract (354 mm in length). At 5,250 rpm, the valve opens and switches to the shorter (282 mm) tract, feeding a larger volume of air for higher power output. Typically with VICS, there is a slight but noticeable drop or "valley" in cylinder-filling efficiency at some point in the rpm band. However, Mazda's engine designers included a resonance chamber cast integral with the manifold. At around 3,000 rpm, which is a critical transitional period, the resonance chamber is connected with the plenum chamber, generating a resonance charge effect, nicely filling the valley for the coming power rise.

Sounds of Miata Music

The Miata design and development engineers gathered at an overnight session at the Miyoshi Proving Ground. A lecturer was invited, Mazda's audio specialist, to examine the sound qualities of various sports cars. He delivered, "A single child's disharmony could easily stand out among 30 kindergarten children's beautiful choir making the total effort discordant. It's not the sound level of the 30, but the total quality of it that makes it pleasant to listeners."

He went on to analyze the competing sports car sounds: the MGF melodically goes *do-mi-so*. The Fiat Barchetta emits *do-do-do*, a bit on the loud side but consistently pleasant. The incumbent Miata's sounds are *do-mi-fa*, with one discordant note spoiling the effort. He recorded the sounds in his pride-and-joy equipment, got rid of the "bad" note from the Miata's exhaust, and, suddenly, it was great music!

Now the engineers went to their operating table — the bench — cutting, welding, testing silencers, and repeating the sequence many times over, much to the horror of their muffler suppliers. Eventually, they arrived at three basic silencer types: manual transmission, automatic and European model, the latter subject to more stringent noise regulations. The sound levels are lowered in all versions, removing the engine's secondary- and fourth-order noises, while emphasizing low-frequency sounds.

Sweet Sixteen

The original Miata was powered by the type B6 1597-cc unit. It was re-introduced in the European MX-5 to power an entry-

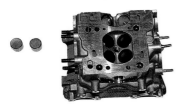

Four-valves-per-cylinder combustion chamber. Mechanical inverted bucket tappets replace the previous hydraulic tappets.

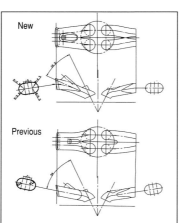

New and old cylinder head designs.

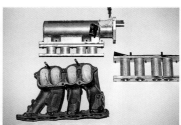

BP's intake port is larger and more upright.

BP 1.8-liter engine with Variable Inertia Charge System (VICS).

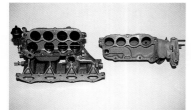

Variable Inertia Charge System is the answer to low- and mid-range torque and high-speed power.

VICS tracts with control valves.

A part of the experimental intake manifold collection.

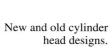

Many intake manifold designs were tried, including these cast and machined ones. The cast manifold surfaces are smoothed by epoxy filling.

Resonance chambers of various volumes were also evaluated.

Type B6 engine is an updated version of the original 1600 unit, which shares features with the BP 1.8, except VICS.

model, which also received a favorable insurance rating in certain countries because of its under 90-bhp classification. For the new MX-5, Mazda decided to use this engine in the Japanese market as well, at the same time restoring and raising its performance.

The engineers' goal was simple: exceed the performance of the original 1600. Their time limit was the end of 1996. They were skeptical, as they had a bigger rabbit to chase — the tuning and refinement of the mainstream BP 1.8 engine. "Going after another rabbit," as the Japanese saying goes, "may spoil the whole hunt."

They would give it a try, installing the camshafts from an all-wheel-drive Familia (Protegé/323), and see how it would go. It went rather sweetly in an engineering mule based on the incumbent roadster. Given a new intake and exhaust system, more efficient mechanical tappets, and a knock-sensor in the ignition system, there was promise of a sweet sixteen reborn.

IMPROVING BENCH-MARK TRANSMISSION AND ADDING NEW ONES

Eliminate Cold Morning Balk

If you are a chief engineer in charge of product evaluation and development, you usually get a test car on a warm platter, so to speak. Your engineers would drive it for a couple of laps and make sure it met current design and development specs before submitting it for your appraisal. They would also clearly define any improvements not yet incorporated.

Takashi Takeshita, Mazda's assistant program manager in charge of that function, is accustomed to the pattern of engineering life. But when he bought his first-generation MX-5, he was treated to some heavy balking from the car's bench-mark transmission which had been lauded for its exceptionally precise, short-throw shift quality. "On freezing mornings when lubricant was still thick, you were invariably greeted by a grinding noise as soon as you shifted into second gear."

Osamu Kameda, one of Mazda's young power train designers and engineers, had experienced similar reluctance in hotter circumstances — auto-cross competition — where the indestructible gearbox required arm-wrenching forces during quick shifts. The boss and men alike were determined to improve on the veteran (inherited from the naturally aspirated RX-7s) transmission in its next Miata life.

Modifications were very thorough. The rear extension casing is now a single-piece casting, instead of the previous two-piece, built-up construction, whose shift-control-rod supports exerted frictional resistance. The new rod is also supported by Teflon-coated bushings, as are the three inner shift rails, instead of the previous machined aluminum surface bearings.

Reluctance of the gears to shift smoothly was caused, in large part, by drag torque between the clutch hub sleeve and the gear

chamfer, producing a "double detent." The refined M15M-D gearbox expands on the asymmetrical gear chamfer design used on the second gear of the original Miata's gear train. In the new version, the lack of symmetry between the acceleration and deceleration sides of the chamfer has been doubled, from the previous 0.8 mm to 1.5 mm. This asymmetric chamfer design is applied to 2nd, 3rd and 4th gears.

Previously the shift-lever base sphere was held by a single pin; in the new design, it is located by two pins, eliminating the lever's play during shifting.

Does Miata Needs A 6-speed Gearbox?

That was the question many debated, including Mazda importers outside of Japan. Their initial response was, "No, it doesn't. At least not at the moment." Shiro Yoshioka, program manager for the roadster while it had a temporary home in the company's commercial vehicle center, answered likewise when the transmission team approached him with the idea of a new 6-speed transmission toward the end of 1995.

The young engineers were far from discouraged. They were in touch with an electronic world on the Internet, where they learned that several competitors were developing, or at least planning, such transmissions for sports and sporty cars. Doing it single-handed would require huge expenditures, both in development and manufacturing, which Mazda could ill afford.

Aisin-AI is a transmission specialist in Nagoya, Japan, whose affiliation with Toyota is well known. They were interested in developing a 6-speed unit for front-engine, rear-wheel-drive cars (Toyota had no such model in production or in planning), and approached the transmission team. Yes, the team would be interested. However, they had no budget to contribute to the design and development, yet. Would Aisin be interested in buying an MX-5 for an engineering mule? Yes, they would. Thus began the Y16M-D transmission program.

Shortly, a prototype gearbox was delivered to Mazda, and installed in a factory Miata. Would program manager Yoshioka be interested in driving it. Yes, he would and he did. He wanted the transmission, like *now!* Shoji Oda, Mazda's ace sports car tuner/driver, was more astute. The man with the lightning hands (he has to shift both left- and right-hand-drive models) declared it was hopelessly slow and vague.

The team and Aisin engineers went back to their respective drawing boards and test-benches, and incorporated all the ideas they could summon. A revised version was installed in what Mazda calls a "mechanical prototype," or an engineering mule, for the new-generation MX-5. Again, it could not keep up with Oda's fast shifts. Major internal changes were made and numerous minor improvements were carried out.

The Y16M-D is a brand new transmission, borrowing nothing from the M15M-D 5-speed unit. Its basic design is Aisin, to whom the Mazda team pays great respect, especially in terms of packaging efficiency and mechanical simplification while assuring function, reliability and durability. There are several ingenious approaches to its design, some contributed by Mazda. The whole gearbox fits where the 5-speed nestles, with no modification to the power-plant frame (Thus, it can be installed in any Miata, new or old).

The gearbox employs triple-cone synchros on 1st and 2nd gears, while all other gears have single-cone synchros. The 3rd and 4th synchros are placed on the counter shaft to reduce synchronizing inertia. The asymmetrical chamfer design was also adopted.

Gears are closely spaced with a direct (1.00:1) fifth ratio, which lowers meshing heat generation at very high speeds by as much as 24 degrees Celsius as compared with the 5-speed box in the direct 4th gear.

Light weight was also an important factor. The transmission is housed in a three-piece aluminum casing. The shift forks are cast in aluminum with sheet-steel contacts. Three shift rails perform shifting instead of a more usual 4-rail arrangement in a 6-speed gearbox. The Y16M-D has gained a scant 1.2 kg in weight over the 5-speed unit.

Test chief Takeshita delivered his verdict of the new transmission: "Very good; it's a gratifying experience to shift through the gears."

Shift lever rigidity is improved for precise feel in the M15M-D transmission.

Weight reduction is achieved by a new aluminum part (right) replacing the previous cast iron.

Standard urethane shift knob is shaped to fit the hand more naturally. Test pieces were handcrafted from clay and the final shape was determined after trial-and-error evaluation.

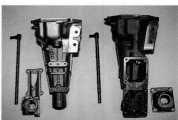

Type-M15M-D 5-speed transmission adopts an integral rear housing, which locates the control rod and shift lever assembly more securely. The previous 2-piece casing is shown at left. The shift rod is now supported by two low-friction Teflon bushings instead of direct aluminum metal contact as in the previous gearbox.

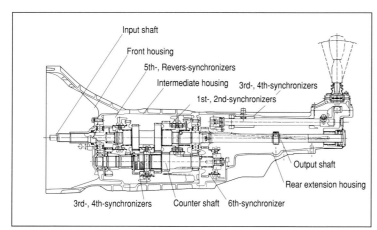

Sectional view of the type-Y16M-D 6-speed transmission.

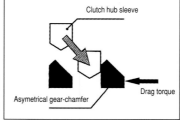

New Aisin-Mazda 6-speed transmission is offered in the Japanese 1800 series. The transmission is held to the same length as the 5-speed unit.

3rd-, 4th- and 6th-gear synchronizers are carried on the counter shaft.

Asymmetrical gear chamfer prevents "double detent" resulting from reluctant engagement of the spline by drag torque. This chamfer design is used for 2nd, 3rd and 4th gears.

Triple-cone synchronizers are used in 1st and 2nd gears to greatly reduce shift effort.

WORKING OUT WITH THE MIATA

"We Carry Over The Cost Factors. But Everything Else Will Be Suited To Purpose."

Shoji Oda knew what he wanted. Oda was a member of Mazda's original "Top Guns," the chassis testing and development team whose members included such outstanding dynamicists as Hirotaka Tachibana, tuner of the original Miata, and Koby Kobayakawa, who was to become the program manager of the RX-7. The first-generation MX-5 chassis had been refined in four major steps, accompanied by several alphabet letters after its development code J58. Oda took part in the latter life of the J58, and knew the chassis's potential had been fully exploited. Its limit was fast being approached.

So Oda's new MX-5 team wanted a new chassis, obviously adhering to the front-engine, rear-drive configuration with a PPF-united drivetrain and all-independent, double-wishbone suspension. Platform carry-over and component sharing was the order of this cost-conscious day. They could carry over the cost factors, they reasoned, while making a new chassis out of the proven design and major components, attaining superior dynamics surpassing the first-generation car, and establishing yet another bench-mark.

Mazda's new product takes shape in the mechanical prototype stage, "Mecha-pro" in the company parlance, into which major components, developed and tested in existing models, on the bench, and nowadays, many in the "tube," are assembled.

Oda's team could not wait for a proper mecha-pro to prove their new chassis concept. Luckily, the department's small fabricating shop was building an MX-5-based engineering mule for the RX-01 rotary-powered concept car for the 1995 Tokyo Motor Show. With the department head's encouragement, the team persuaded the shop's good people to build another conversion, this one incorporating all the ideas they had for a next-generation MX-5: a stiffer body frame, new suspension geometry and elements that were aimed at superior chassis performance, with the potential for greatly improving roadholding, handling and ride comfort. Kouji Tsuji, chassis designer, understood the development team's ideas and objectives, and proceeded to pen — or mouse — the essential ingredients.

The pre-mecha-pro exercise worked extremely well, leading to an "official" fleet of mechanical prototypes utilizing current MX-5 bodies but incorporating new inner body structure,

Mazda calls its engineering mule a "Mechanical Prototype," or for short "Mecha-pro." The new MX-5 innards are hidden within this after-a-fender-bender-looking incumbent roadster.

The MX-5 mechanical prototype on the left. There was even an earlier version, a "Pre-Mecha-pro," a perfectly ordinary-looking Miata modified to the development team's specifications of a new car, hand-built together with the car on the right, which is a different breed of animal all together; a mecha-pro for the 1995 Tokyo auto show, rotary-powered RX-01 concept car. The tubular top simulates a coupe construction.

Bumpers are weighted to simulate the new car's weight distribution.

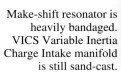

Make-shift resonator is heavily bandaged. VICS Variable Inertia Charge Intake manifold is still sand-cast.

Mazda engineers evaluate the new exhaust system's "music" among friendly competitors at the Miyoshi Proving Ground.

chassis and drivetrain changes and modifications. Some looked ungainly, as if they had just survived a series of freeway fender-and-bumper-benders. One mechanical prototype, more discreetly clothed but its bug-eye headlamps permanently popped up to make room for the new frame structure, covered many miles in Europe, accompanied by several "friendly" competitors as well as a current MX-5.

Most of these prototypes were destined for crash barriers after they served dynamic purposes. Senior development engineer Hiroyoshi Moriyama saved one example, not the pretty European-trip car but an after-fender-bender variety, and let co-author Jack Yamaguchi sample it on the Ujina factory's loop:

"It was not much to look at. Rectangular headlamps just hung there. Bumper reinforcement beams were exposed with no outer skin, but functionally they were weighted properly to simulate the design weight and balance. The interior was stock Miata, except one very nice item which I am not allowed to disclose, but which would appear in a production car in the future.

The 1.8-liter engine revved willingly and happily, as it had obviously been doing under the heavy but expert right feet of its tuners. The improved 5-speed gearbox was delightful, and the clutch's take-up was just right. Development chief Takeshita confessed he had learned an important lesson from a racing-car-like clutch he installed in the AZ-1 micro sports: that clutch was too abrupt because he had only 5 mm of pedal travel before it engaged.

It was the car's handling and straight-line stability that impressed me most, two virtues not necessarily combined in the original MX-5. The car turned-in sharply as you would expect from a Miata; in a sharp bend on either end of the loop it exhibited excellent grip and neutral behavior. Drop down a gear and you could still hang the tail out, but very controllably. Moriyama reminded me that the car was still too heavy. I hardly noticed it. In this case, beauty was certainly more than skin deep."

Tough, Solid Body

Professor Toshihiko Hirai of National Oh-ita University, former program manager of the original MX-5, says that car's strength was in its straight-through longitudinal frame and highly rigid central tunnel construction, the latter acting as a backbone structure to which major underfloor frames were securely attached. This basic structure has been carried over in the new Miata. There were some concessions, however, in the original body shell, mainly for the sake of light weight, because Hirai was a stickler to gram details.

Over the years, Hiroshi Yamamoto and Takao Kijima, program managers for the first-generation's latter life, endeavored to strengthen the body and chassis, to reduce noise,

The mechanical prototype was sent to Europe in more respectable clothing. Headlamps are permanently popped up to accommodate the new inner structure.

Front and rear airdam extensions simulate the new car's aerodynamics.

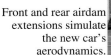

A recent drive in a U.S. spec mecha-pro turned out to be quite a pleasant experience with a very willing engine, a supple ride and agile handling, although the windows did not roll down.

Oopt, watch out, it's the new 6-speed gearbox in a mechanical prototype.

vibration and harshness. First, a brace bar was added, tying the tops of the rear suspension towers together. Lateral brace bars were added to tie the subframes, with rear longitudinal bars tying the rear subframe to the body shell.

Kijima considered additional strength-enhancing measures, but found that further modifications would not be cost-, weight- or function-effective. His design team would, therefore, concentrate on the design and development of a next-generation body.

Program manager Hirai of the first-generation Miata had to rely heavily on the company's computer analytical ability, because he could not get enough human resources in the early stages of design. The Dynamic Modal Analysis applied to the MX-5 was the most extensive at the time, beginning with the early mechanical prototype design which had 1,350 nodal points for stress measurement, progressing rapidly to a then-record 8,900 points in the final production version.

A simplified analytical model of the Finite Element Method used in the new MX-5 design had 9,000 nodal points, and the final detailed version 30,000! Computer-aided engineering greatly assisted strengthening of the body shell via strategically placed reinforcements and heavier-gauge sheet metal, while holding weight increases to a minimum. The new car's body-in-white, including doors and lids, weighs 272 kg (598 lb), versus the previous model's 262 kg (576 lb), a truly remarkable achievement when one considers the car's improved rigidity and more stringent crash requirements, including Europe's 40-percent off-set, deformable barrier frontal crash, and the U.S., European and Japanese side impact tests.

While the new body's static rigidity improvements may seem small, 1.3 percent in torsion and 7.6 percent in bending, its dynamic torsional rigidity, measured at the lower A-pillar zone, has improved by 35 percent as compared with the first-generation body.

Mazda's designers and engineers must have examined those thousands of parts and components that make up the Miata with a fine-tooth comb, some microscopes and metallurgical instruments to reduce weight, while preserving, and in many cases improving, various functions. One example is the new soft top, which is 1.3 kg (2.9 lb) lighter than the previous

S1 is the prototype that looks and acts (supposedly, sometimes) like the production car. The designation is actually a misnomer as there is no longer an S2 or later prototypes, thanks largely to modern computer analysis and simulation.

A batch of S1s were hand-built in Mazda's prototype shop.

Key members of the MX-5 design and development team with an S1: program manager Kijima, second from left, with assistant managers Munenori Yamaguchi and Nobuyuki Nakanishi in the foreground.

Shoji Oda, development engineer/driver (in black jacket) checks suspension settings during S1 build.

Program manger Kijina and his lieutenant Yamaguchi fitting the "world's best ragtop" on an S1.

New MX-5 features a glass rear window with heated elements for defrosting/demisting, yet it is lighter in weight than the previous soft top with plastic window.

Elaborate sealing elements ensure tight weather protection.

version, despite having a glass rear window instead of a plastic one.

The original Miata soft top received high praise, for its one-hand ease of operation, and its good weather protection. Enter the venerable development chief Takashita, who used to hose down his own Miata. The only difference was he clamped the end of the water-hose in his powerful hand, building up and shooting a high-pressure jet of water at the top and the windows. He declared the new car's top must seal against such abuse.

New Miatas coming off the Ujina assembly line are spot-checked in a monsoon chamber, where they are subjected to a downpour which, according to a senior production engineer, could not occur naturally on this planet. A word of caution. You may notice very thin lips on the seal ends that may appear left by casting molds. Do not cut these pieces off. They are important functional parts of the sealing.

WEIGHT REDUCTION

BODY	ITEM	WEIGHT SAVED (kg)
Headlamp units	Fixed and integrated lamps	5.56
Rear bumper	Single piece facia	1.49
Rear bumper reinforcement	Extruded aluminum	0.80
Soft top	Light gauge frame	1.30
Hood	Light gauge inner panel	0.77
Front bumper	Polypropylene facia	0.43
Central floor panel	Lighter gauge steel	0.39
Rear suspension tower bar	Discontinued	2.20
CHASSIS		
Tire x 4 (195/15 size)	New design	2.40
Shock absorber mounting	Separate mounting	1.50
Rear lateral bracebar	New design	0.57
Steering gear	Smaller unit	0.18
Steering shaft	Hollow shaft	0.17
ELECTRICAL		
Meters and gauges	Electronic drive	0.31
License plate lamp	Smaller unit	0.16
Horn	Smaller unit	0.24
ENGINE		
Starting motor	Reduction mechanism	1.4
Tappets	Mechanical	0.80
Crankshaft angle sensor	Smaller unit	0.21
Secondary resonator*	Eliminated	0.20
Air-cleaner	Mount bracket	0.08
Cylinder-head cover	New design	0.05
Alternator bracket	Altered design	0.03
Camshafts	New design	0.02
Radiator side support	Eliminated	1.45
Air-conditioning compressor	Scroll-type	0.75
Air mount bracket	Aluminum	1.10
INTERIOR		
Seat	Inner structure	2.40
Air condenser	Integrated receiver-tank	1.05
Air cooling unit	New design	0.40
Heating core	Aluminum	0.20

Note:* U.S. and Japanese models

"Are You Sure We Created A Miata?"

Development engineer Oda was not happy with the S1, the first hand-assembled prototype that looked like and was supposed to perform like the new MX-5.

It looked fine, but did not perform to the development team's expectations. The engine did not respond. Apparently the induction system's volume downstream of the throttle was acting as a damper. As soon as the right foot was pressed, there was a delay of a good half a second, literally diluting the car's

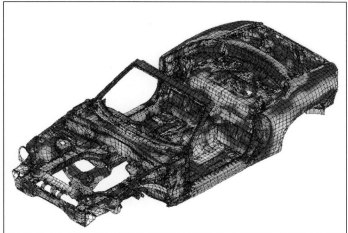

Lightweight high-rigidity body was designed with and developed using Mazda's extensive analytical and simulation techniques.

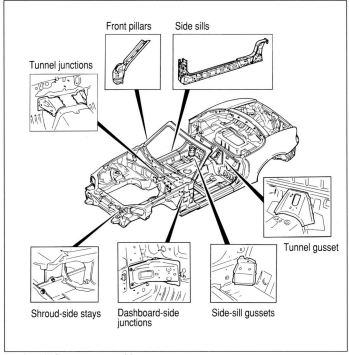

Body reinforcements and braces.

performance. The smaller B6 suffered the most. An engine development engineer shudders, "The summer of 1997 was hell. The chassis improved greatly (Oda had a serious reservation about that, too), but the engine was inhaling too much hot air. The air intake was re-routed, and a heat shield was installed near the radiator. Cooling air was properly directed via twin counter-rotating electric fans. We burned a lot of midnight oil. Then came the winter, and melted snow got into the engine compartment."

Development chief Takeshita was optimistic: "That's the difference between the bench, the tube and the real world. The induction system was essentially developed in the former, and literally shoehorned into the S1's engine bay. In the process, it was awkwardly bent in the restrictive space. It was to be expected, and would presently be rectified."

The chassis designers had been happy with the mechanical prototype's combination of stability and agility. However, Mazda's U.S. and European development engineers had long been pounding on them for improved high-speed, straight-line stability, and less on-center "twitchiness," which was often misinterpreted as a lack of stability. So the designers decided to take advantage of the chassis' newly gained capabilities, and switched to a 17.0:1 steering ratio instead of the previous 15.0:1.

Oda did not like it, bluntly asking, "Have we created a Miata or a plain touring car?" Development chief Takeshita was concerned, too, although he did not voice it loudly. His role at that early stage was to encourage the designers and engineers to improve the S1. Takeshita later offered Jack Yamaguchi a chance to drive one of the early S1s, to illustrate the team's subsequent efforts and the fruits of their labor of love:

"It was a cold morning at Miyoshi, with snow banks on either side of the course. I was grateful for the Wind Blocker, as Takeshita insisted I should drive the car with the top down. The S1's engine was by then breathing nicely, thanks to the engine team's hard work, and felt like it was putting out an honest 140 bhp.

The improved 5-speed gearbox was terrific. I still rate it the very best of any sports car transmission, including Mazda's own brand-new 6-speed unit (Takeshita disagrees with me on this point.).

The new body shell's stiffness was a quantum leap beyond the first-generation MX-5, and little shake was transmitted. The suspension soaked up a myriad of bumps and the car gripped various surfaces tenaciously. The Miyoshi test track, especially the winding Alpine section, could be treacherous with melted snow running across parts of it. The car's handling was extremely stable, but not as razor-edge-sharp as the original Miata's. It took me back to the summer of 1983...

I was accompanying Mazda's development team of the

second-generation RX-7, including engineer Hirotaka Tachibana, to the hallowed Nurburgring in Germany, with an X1 mechanical prototype in the guise of a first-generation '7. In those days, Mazda built a series of mechanical prototypes, X0, X1 and X2, then moved thorough S1 and S2 prototypes during development. The X1 was equipped with a new rear suspension, a product of the fertile mind of chassis designer *extraordinaire,* Takao Kijima, now the program manager of the new Miata. The independent suspension was a variation of the semi-trailing-arm system with reactive toe-control and camber-compensating functions.

The X1 prototype was the most forgiving car among those compared. In this early stage of development, the rear suspension assumed immediate stabilizing toe-in upon the first sign of lateral acceleration, and generated exceptional cornering forces, combined with good straight-line stability. However, the steering was insensitive to steering inputs, almost approaching dullness. Set the car up for a mid-speed corner, wiggle the steering wheel, and nothing happened. The car proceeded unperturbed, as if the rear suspension had a mind of its own. Tachibana did not approve of this handling trait.

There was a minor drama on the Ring. A team member 'lost' the 944 in a big way and bent it, on the first lap after switching from the X1. He must have been taken by the German car's initial understeer followed by an abrupt lift-off oversteer on a tricky reverse-camber bend. Fortunately, I drove the Porsche first, with due respect and care, then switched to the X1.

History did not repeat itself, and I did not bend a Miata. When I switched to a production first-generation car after driving the S1, I knew it wouldn't be as forgiving as the S1, so I was prepared to apply opposite lock as soon as the rear end tried to catch up with the front. But isn't this a part of the fun of Miata driving? And I loved the original car's quick 15.0:1 steering."

Chassis designer Kouji Tsuji was not surprised at Oda's and Takeshita's reaction to the early S1's "benign" character. "That was a happy miscalculation on our part; the car's stability was still well proven. Some people within the camp were, however, quite vocal, suggesting we should go back to the first-generation's handling. But I knew we were on the right track. Agility could be built in, and nicely combined with the car's superior handling and stability. It was a gratifying and promising starting point for development."

Westward, Ho! To Europe and the Coast

The S1 promptly reverted to the 15.0:1 steering ratio, and chassis refinements and modifications were carried out. In the month of May, 1997, the S1 went to Europe, accompanied by a development team headed by senior engineer Shinro Kinoshita and Mazda R&D Europe's evaluation team. It joined up with its "friendly" competitors: two BMW Z3s, a Fiat Barchetta, an MGF and a production MX-5 1.8 for a dash across the Continent. Program manager Kijima joined the troops toward the end of the tour.

The evaluating team rated the S1 highly, and it easily surpassed its competitors in three major areas: 1) Spirited and stable handling characteristics combined with good ride quality; 2) Improved interior comfort, including a marked reduction in body vibration and wind noise; 3) Improved high-rpm, high-speed performance realized by the more powerful engine.

The European team had to take the car up to its maximum, 200 km/h (125 mph), and sustain this speed when traffic was clear on the Autobahnen. Its straight-line stability was praised by the testers. Handling on twisty roads received high marks, the joint team declaring BIC — Best in Class.

The European contingent pointed out that the BP engine's torque characteristics had improved from the mechanical prototype's noticeable "valley," which occurred between 2,000 and 4,000 rpm. This had been narrowed down to a 1,000-rpm range.

Another Mazda development team, headed by senior development engineer Moriyama, joined Koby Kobayakawa's California group in the spring of 1997 for an extensive evaluation of the S1. They reported similar findings on the engine's torque characteristics during acceleration from a corner apex with 1/8 to 3/4 throttle valve opening. It was to receive Hiroshima's attention and improvement.

As for the S1 car's handling, roadholding and ride quality, Europeans and Americans heaped praises upon it. Shoji Oda was confident of the design and development team's achievements. Describing the new Miata's ride, he says, "Remove the seat from the new car and sit on the floor. You feel about the same vibration level as sitting on the seat of the first-generation car!"

They were as thorough in their evaluation and demand for tire performance. Michelin's Pilot SX GT passed the team's rigorous tests with flying colors, and was promptly made standard foot-wear for U.S. and Japanese performance models. However, a well-known brand did not meet the American evaluation team's exacting criteria on rain-grooved freeway surfaces and was excluded from the initial equipment.

The development team decided on a single optimized suspension specification for the world, including spring rates, shock absorber damping characteristics, bump stoppers, anti-roll bar diameters and pivot bushings. Additionally, the U.S. and Japanese ranges would offer a Sports suspension: the American Sports Package and the Japanese RS with firmer settings, including Bilstein shock absorbers.

Mazda's home team continued the Miata work-out, incorporating numerous improvements sought by the European and American groups, as well as its own astute engineers. Road impressions by author John Dinkel attest to the fruits of their tremendous efforts. The Miata is once again BIC.

Rear bulkhead/tunnel reinforcement.

Fuel tank is positioned under this box member.

The MX-5's body strength is largely a result of the straight-through frame members.

Front bulkhead/tunnel braces.

Front suspension is by double-wishbones. The lower and upper arms are attached to a fabricated steel subframe, which also carries the front part of the united power plant and the steering gear assembly.

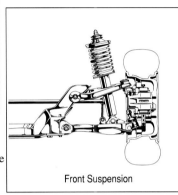

Front Suspension

Twin impact bars in each door extend into the door's front and rear ends where they overlap with the body for added strength against side impact.

Spare wheel well.

Rear suspension is also by double wishbones. The subframe carries the suspension and the rear of the power plant. The subframe is reinforced by lateral and longitudinal brace bars. The front ends of the longitudinal bars are attached to the body shell, adding to the subframe's structural rigidity.

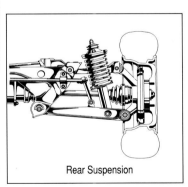

Rear Suspension

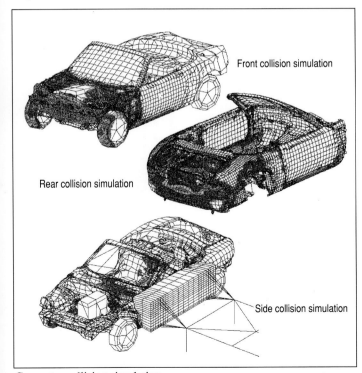

Front collision simulation

Rear collision simulation

Side collision simulation

Computer collision simulation.

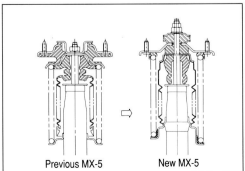

Previous MX-5   New MX-5

Coil spring and shock absorber top mounts are separate.

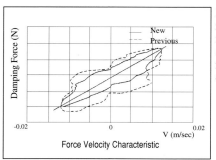

Force Velocity Characteristic

Frictional interference is reduced by the separate top mounts, contributing to smoother and more responsive shock absorber damping characteristics.

Assistant program manager Takashi Takeshita receives the first S1 while craftsmen from the prototype shop look on.

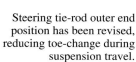

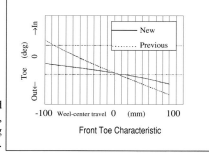

Front Toe Characteristic

Steering tie-rod outer end position has been revised, reducing toe-change during suspension travel.

New suspension subframe brace bar is straight and bolted at four points. Previous "bent" brace bar is bolted at two points.

Response of Yaw Rate in Slalom Test

Slalom test at 100 km/h indicates the new car's improved response to steering input (data obtained with Sports suspension package).

Rear lateral brace bar is also straight. Previous bent brace bar.

Response of Lateral and Longitudial Acceleration Handling course

The new car possesses improved controllability at the limit of adhesion.

Transitional body roll is much smoother during reversals of steering input.

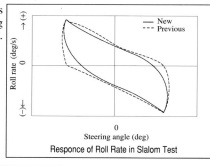

Responce of Roll Rate in Slalom Test

The new MX-5 is less prone to suspension bottoming, as indicated in this test on Mazda's bottoming evaluation stretch driven at 60 km/h.

"Hands-off" stability recovery is improved while lateral acceleration and yaw-rate peak values are higher.

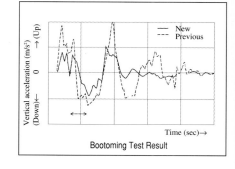

Bootoming Test Result

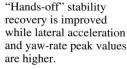

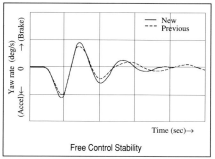

Free Control Stability

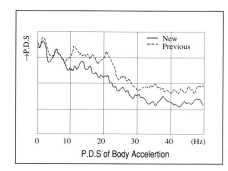

P.D.S of Body Accelertion

Power density spectrum (PDS) test indicates a marked reduction in body acceleration, especially in the critical 15-30 Hz frequency range, contributing to superior ride.

Author Jack Yamaguchi's early outing in an S1 on the Miyoshi Global Road Course.

S1 goes to Europe with a bra.

Among "friendly" competitors in Europe.

Yamaguchi discusses the early S1's too-benign handling characteristics with development chief Takashi Takeshita. Takeshita will add more agility to the MX-5's excellent roadholding.

Mazda's European R&D engineers join the Japanese team.

Mazda's sports car tuners, the test and development team. From left: Shoji Oda, Hiroyoshi Moriyama, Nobuhiro Yamamoto, Katsuhiro Moro, Takashi Takeshita and Shinro Kinoshita.

Speedo needle is passing 190 km/h (119 mph), with 10 more to come.

Program manager Takao Kijima with an S1 in Europe.

American R&D team finds every worse road surfaces in California.

S1 goes to America.

Fine-tuning the suspension on Ortega Highway wayside.

Miata people in Hiroshima.

A naked early production Miata being put through it paces for final validation.

Kelvin Hiraishi, MRA's development engineer at the wheel.

Irvine, California, team.

Sports car country and sports car weather. California, here we come!

MX-5 Miata Production

Body-in-white welding.

Front suspension/subframe build-up.

Rear suspension/subframe assembly.

Final power train assembly stage. This one has an automatic transmission.

Miata assembly and power train assembly are on mixed lines. A Miata inline power unit is followed by a transverse one.

Vehicle assembly.

Power train/suspension are attached, while the rear assembly awaits.

Aligning the power plant frame with this bar jig.

Soft top is installed.

This cut-up car is for training pur-poses. Parts of the car that are critical for precise welding and assembling works are highlighted.

Each car is put through a shower booth for leak check. Water containing a fluorescent element shows up under ultra-violet light.

This is not just a shower but more like a monsoon, downpouring 3,000 liters of water per hour. Completed cars are randomly tested in this chamber.

Spot checks are performed on this shaker rig which simulates bad road surfaces.

A short burst of speed on the Ujina factory's loop completes the test cycle.

Chapter

3

THE FIRST-GENERATION

HOW IT ALL BEGAN

It was November 1983 when Mazda launched a program that was given a curious sounding name, "Offline 55." It was the Hiroshima-based automobile manufacturer's first serious look into the future since its miraculous recovery from a near debacle after the Great Energy Crises. Mazda had by then steadied itself after the severe buffeting, and had a well defined line of "mainstream" products, such as the 323, 626 and 929 cars and small commercial vehicle series. These models were on regular model cycles.

Michinori Yamanouchi, then managing director in charge of product planning and development, feared that the regained stability might lead to complacency, with his planners, designers and engineers too preoccupied with their evolutionary development of these known "mainstream" qualities. Mazda was in dire need of moving into the future. So Yamanouchi set up a small advance team within his engineering organization to probe "offline" projects free of the existing product boundaries. Yamanouchi was inspired by the late Soichiro Honda's daring philosophy, encouraging his engineers to tackle challenges with as little as a 10-percent success ratio. Obviously, Mazda's management would expect more; even Honda of the 1980s wouldn't have been content with that small a level of success. So Yamanouchi set the team's goal at 55 percent "do-ability," accepting a 45-percent risk ratio. And the Japanese word for "5-5" rhymes nicely with "Go-Go."

Several candidates were put forth, some very interesting, including a 323 convertible and a pocket-size sports car (both to be produced in small numbers later), a cross-over on/off-road sports car, an executive sports sedan, a mini "space wagon," and a rotary-powered pickup. The planners assigned to the program preferred, unequivocally, what they called LWS, an acronym for "Light-Weight Sports car," over the other proposals.

Early in the following year, 1984, the planners in Japan and the company's California research center threw themselves into deciding the preliminary configuration of the LWS. They had three types to consider: the front-wheel-drive configuration predominant among the world's small cars, the midship-engine layout favored by racing and exotic car enthusiasts for superior dynamics, and the classic front-engine, rear-wheel-drive model that had propelled many a famed sports car throughout automotive history.

Styling proposals for the three configurations were consigned to two design studios outside Mazda headquarters in Hiroshima. One was the Product Planning and Research Division of the then-Mazda North America, Inc. in Irvine, California. The other was a small studio in Mazda's Tokyo headquarter building, which was to become the nucleus of the Technical Research Center in nearby Yokohama. These two design branches were modest establishments, no more than one-room studios, but they had a handful of young designers and planners brimming with enthusiasm to conceive and shape Mazda's cars of tomorrow.

The Tokyo studio chose the front-wheel-drive and midship-engine approaches, the former to become a "CRX killer," and the latter its ace in the hole, the closest thing to a pukka racing car and the smallest such model. Little did Tokyo know that Toyota was preparing such a model, the MR2, with exactly the same wheelbase and height!

The California contingent chose the front-engine, rear-wheel-drive configuration without the slightest hesitation. And their car would be an open-bodied roadster, for them, LWS standing for "Lithesome, Wind-in-the-face, Sports car."

The two studios began their work in earnest, first with sketches, followed by drawings, and finally life-size clay models, leading to fiberglass mockups. In the meantime, the planning and engineering group evaluated the three configurations. They had earlier built a mid-engine car using a 323 body and racing-type suspension, which displayed "fantastic handling and agility," said a leading member, "but soon that monster-enemy, NVH (noise, vibration and harshness), raised its ugly head."

Toward the end of 1984, a year after the inception of the LWS project as a part of the Offline 55 Program, the front-engine, rear-wheel-drive roadster emerged as the winner.

1990 Mazda MX-5 Miata.

1990 Mazda MX-5 Miata U.S. version with driver-side SRS airbag.

Program manager Masakatsu Kato did not want the LWS project — code-named P729 — to end as an exercise in styling and product concept. By that time, Mazda's separate Technical Center had been established to further the studies and research into the future. The P729 was transferred to the new advance center accompanied by Kato, who exploited one of the Tech Center's research activities, the feasibility study of plastic-bodied cars, which was stimulated by GM's rush toward such construction with the Corvette and the space-frame Fiero.

Britain's International Automotive Design (IAD) was commissioned to engineer and build a running prototype based on the P729 styling design. It was given the code V705, conveying yet another cautious message that it was still very much a research project. This single example of the V705 was brought back to Japan, via Santa Barbara, California, for a day's outing on the town's scenic roads in October 1985, to probe its presence in the country where the planners felt it would belong. As later events unfolded, more than one half of

Three fiberglass proposals gather in Hiroshima's viewing hall in September 1984.

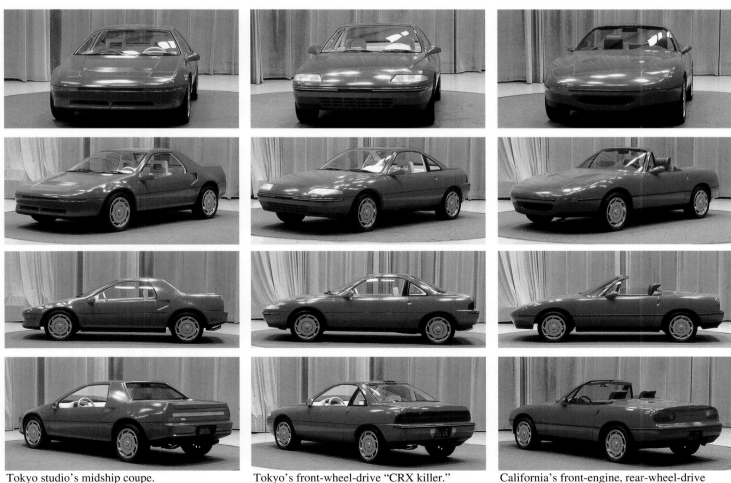

Tokyo studio's midship coupe.

Tokyo's front-wheel-drive "CRX killer."

California's front-engine, rear-wheel-drive roadster.

the first-generation MX-5 Miata's production was to be destined for America.

STILL THE ONE

While the V705 was being built in England, Mazda's North American design studio began working on the second full-size design model in the P729 project, which was completed in early December 1985. A month later, serious studies began on the product feasibility of the LWS. Mazda's product development apparatus was now in gear.

P729 program manager Masakatsu Kato, however, elected to stay with the Technical Center to pursue his favorite future projects. A new manager was urgently required. Toshihiko Hirai, then the design leader of the mainstream 323 small sedan/hatchback series, responded to the call and was heartily endorsed by Kato. No one in the company's engineering hierarchy would be better qualified than Hirai, whose technical and organizational skills were well-recognized and respected.

Hirai, as well as Kato, knew that while the LWS's basic concept was sound and promising, the V705's steel backbone frame and plastic body were not necessarily the best weight and cost combination for a series production car. Hirai would have to start from a clean sheet of paper to build his new LWS around an all-steel, welded unit body. His predicament was that he was not provided with enough human resources to execute all that clean paper work — blueprints, to be exact — required to design an automobile!

Mazda's engineering division was then in a maddening product rush to launch new products, mainstream as well as proposed new vehicles. These included the people-hauler MPV and a new "K car," a micro runabout Mazda had abandoned years ago but whose return was fervently sought by Japanese dealers. Hirai won the LWS appointment, but, unfortunately, few engineering-designers were assigned to his project from the product development side of the company. So he recruited a handful of research designers from the Technical Center where the P729 had originated, and installed them in a small office by the river that flows along the main Hiroshima R&D and factory complex. The bare room was promptly named "Riverside Suite." At least the LWS had the nucleus of a proper design and development team.

Hirai was one of Mazda's pioneer engineers who recognized the power of the computer in design and engineering, and that was the tool he provided to his small team. Mazda's analytical program had by then progressed to GNC-2 (Geometric-modeling and Numerical Control 2), and was to move onto the third generation, whose full force was applied to the creation of the MX-5's body largely in the "tube," eliminating much paperwork and expediting development, so that the design would glide through its time table to the car's fruition. In

DMA (Dynamic Modal Analysis), a test body was placed on a shaker rig and put through vibrations of varying frequencies and magnitudes. Such dynamic testing and analysis were more informative than static ones, greatly accelerating the car's development.

The IAD-built V705 had to make do with a proprietary SOHC 1.4-liter 4-cylinder engine from the rear-wheel-drive GLC/323, as well as suspension from an old RX-7 and a 929 Sedan. These were totally inadequate for the new sports car's performance and refinement. It would be totally new from the ground up, as no suitable platform existed within the company's product lineup. The power unit had to come from the corporate parts bins, as it was by far the most expensive component to tool for, and a new engine would not have been

V705 running prototype engineered and built by Britain's International Automotive Design (IAD) on the California design theme. Research engineer Itsuo Ishida ready to embark on his first run while the late John Shute of IAD looks on.

V705 has a backbone frame and plastic body. The engine is a carburetted SOHC 1.4-liter inline four from a GLC wagon.

Interior design is by IAD.

V705 takes a circuitous trip back to Japan via Santa Barbara, California, where the roadster's product viability is confirmed.

justified for the production volume envisaged. A promising candidate was the type B6 1.6-liter engine, a double-overhead-camshaft, 16-valve, electronic fuel injection unit that powered a performance version of the 323 front-wheel-drive series.

When Hirai's design team turned this engine 90 degrees to install it longitudinally and "front-midship" in the new sports car, they promptly hit a snag, literally. The ignition distributor was sticking out of the rear and the engine like a sore thumb, interfering with the firewall. The power-train division's chief came to Hirai's rescue, asking him if he would allocate an extra 10,000 yen per car, quite a large expenditure on Hirai's tight budget, on a crankshaft angle sensor which would nicely squeeze into the available space, and would dispense with the distributor. Along with the sensor, Hirai got a fully electronic ignition system.

The tuning of the type B6 engine was much like that of the body shell: not enough manpower. Hirai persisted and persuaded the power train group that, "This is one engine that would carry the largest MAZDA name on its camcover (many volume production engines had to assume dual identities, for OEM supplies, and thus remain anonymous)." Heavy midnight oil was burnt, transforming this basically sedan engine into a willing, high-revving sports car unit, earning a unique suffix, "ZE." The B6-ZE was now revving happily to a 7,000-limit.

There was one thing left undone, Hirai regrets today. He was aware the engine had a limitation because of its ductile cast iron crankshaft. However, it could still be extended by several hundred more rpm, had it been fitted with a lighter-weight flywheel. This was denied on the grounds that it would have adversely affected the engine's low-speed running and its exhaust emissions. The MX-5 had to wait for its second update in 1995 when a lighter flywheel was adopted for the BP-ZE 1.8-liter engine, accompanied by a higher-capacity electronic control unit (ECU) that took care of the engine's high-end power, exhaust cleansing, and stabilized the engine's low-speed characteristics.

The all-new suspension, by classic "double wishbones," or unequal-length upper-and-lower-A-arms fore and aft, was designed by Mazda's chassis designer *extraodinaire*, Takao Kijima, creator of the second- and third-generation RX-7 suspensions. Kijima was to become the program manager for the new MX-5 Miata. Interestingly, it was the chassis design group which advocated the adoption of a frame that would tie the power unit and the final drive together to form an integral power plant. The first batch of M-1 (Mechanical prototype 1) cars did not have this feature. The idea was to integrate the drive train so that it would respond to the driver's commands more quickly and accurately, as well as widely spreading the assembly's mounting points, preventing axle-windup on spirited takeoff and acceleration. An elaborately shaped, aluminum PPF (Power Plant Frame) was designed and fitted.

The Mazda MX-5, named "Miata" for the U.S.A., under the internal product code J58G, made its debut at the Chicago Auto Show in February 1989, and was launched in America in April of the same year. Mazda was then pursuing its grand marketing strategies in Japan with five dealer networks, riding on the rapidly inflating "bubble" economy of the time.

The sports car was given to one of them, Eunos, and called "Eunos Roadster." It was introduced in September 1989. Sales in Australia and Europe began in October of the same year and February of 1990, respectively, under the name "Mazda MX-5," sans Miata.

Final design model of the MX-5.

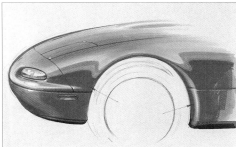

Wu-Huang Chin refines the third-stage design of the P729/J58G project.

A worldly wisdom observes that success has many fathers, and failure is often orphaned. Toshihiko Hirai was the true father of the first-generation MX-5 Miata. In all fairness, Masakatsu Kato was the father of its forerunner P729 and a lone offspring, the V705.

After the birth of the MX-5, Hirai fathered yet another unusual project, this one really an orphan conceived in the company's expansive marketing scheme. But few in the engineering hierarchy took it seriously, let alone willingly shepherd it through the rigors of development.

This model was the AZ-1 micro. In the face of Honda's comeback in this segment, Mazda's dealers had long been pressing management to bring back light cars.

However, Mazda's human and material resources were stretched to the limit in the onrush of new products during the Great Bubble period, so Mazda management negotiated with Suzuki to supply a front-wheel-drive platform. It was this car, sans bodywork, to which Mazda grafted the running gear from its new light runabout Carol. The drivetrain was moved behind the two seats and Mazda stylists sculptured a cute 2-door body to create the tiny, mid-engine, gull-wing AZ-1 sports cars.

It was this turbocharged micro projectile which marketers injected into the new Mazda Autozam (*Maz*-auto backward) dealership network to generate showroom traffic. Unfortunately, none of the micro sports cars from Mazda, Honda (mid-engine Beat) and Suzuki (the front-engine rear-drive Cappuccino) fared well in the ensuing Japanese economy largely of their petite sizes and relative high prices.

The redoubtable Hirai concedes some glaring shortcomings of the hastily developed AZ-1. However, he never hides the fact that he fathered it. Hirai retired from Mazda, and is now professor of the engineering department of National Oh-ita University in the southern island of Kyushu, imparting his wisdom to his favorite subject, "Sensibility Engineering."

Program manager Toshihiko Hirai in the cockpit of the first S1 prototype while development engineer Hirotaka Tachibana and vehicle designer Masaaki Watanabe look on.

B6-ZE engine and type-M 5-speed transmission. The engine was transplanted from the 323 performance model, turned 90 degrees and tuned for the sports car.

Chassis is all new with classical double-wishbone suspension, rack-and-pinion steering and four-wheel disc brakes.

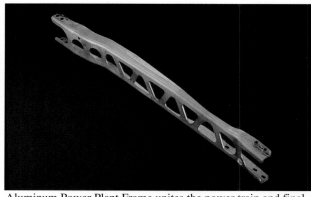

Aluminum Power Plant Frame unites the power train and final drive.

J58G makes its first public appearance at the Chicago auto show in February 1989. It is called Mazda MX-5 Miata for America and launched in May 1989, followed by Canadian introduction a month later.

In Japan, the car is assigned to the newly created Eunos dealer network, called the Eunos Roadster, and introduced in September 1989.

EVOLUTION OF THE MX-5 MIATA/ROADSTER

1989 (1990 Model Year) J58G Series

Chronology:

February 1989
— Debut at the Chicago Auto Show

May 1989
— U.S. launch; fitted with driver-side SRS airbag as standard equipment.

June 1989
— Canadian launch.

September 1989
— Japanese launch as Eunos Roadster.

October 1989
— Australian launch as MX-5.

October 1989
— British Racing Green exterior/Tan interior concept car shown at the Tokyo Motor Show.

February 1990
— European launch begins in U.K. and Netherlands.

Mechanical changes and options:
— Optional viscous-type limited-slip differential
— Optional removable hardtop (in Red only)

1989 (1990 Model Year) J58G MX-5 Miata
SPECIFICATIONS AND PERFORMANCE (U.S. model)

DIMENSIONS AND WEIGHTS
External Dimensions

Overall Length	in. (mm)	155.4 (3,948)
Overall Width	in. (mm)	65.9 (1,676)
Overall Height	in. (mm)	48.2 (1,224)
Wheelbase	in. (mm)	89.2 (2,266)
Track, front	in. (mm)	55.5 (1,410)
rear	in. (mm)	56.2 (1,428)
Ground Clearance (laden)	in. (mm)	4.5 (115)

Internal Dimensions

Front Leg Room	in. (mm)	42.7 (1,085)
Head Room with top closed	in. (mm)	37.1 (942)
Shoulder Room	in. (mm)	50.4 (1,280)
Accelerator Pedal-Rear Hip Point	in. (mm)	43.0 (1,093)
Vehicle Weight in U.S.A base	lbs. (kg)	2,116 (960)
with "A" option package	lbs. (kg)	2,182 (990)
with "B" option package	lbs. (kg)	2,189 (993)
in Canada base	lbs. (kg)	2,116 (960)
with option package	lbs. (kg)	2,125 (964)
Weight Distribution, front/rear (unladen)		52/48

ENGINE

Type		Inline 4-cylinder, water-cooled, DOHC, 4- valves per cylinder
Bore x Stroke	in. (mm)	3.1 x 3.3 (78 x 83.6)
Total Displacement	cu in. (cc)	97.45 (1597)
Compression Ratio		9.4:1

Maximum Power, SAE net	bhp (kw)	116 (86) @ 6,500 rpm
Maximum Torque, SAE net	lb-ft (Nm)	100 (135) @ 5,500 rpm
Fuel system		Electronic Gasoline Injection (EGI)
Fuel Requirement		Unleaded regular (over 91 RON)
Cylinder Block		Cast iron
Cylinder Head		Die-cast aluminum
Piston		Die-cast aluminum
Crankshaft		Ductile cast iron, with eight counterweights
Number of Main Bearings		5
Camshaft Layout		Double Overhead
Camshaft Drive		Cogged belt
Valve Acting Mechanism		Via hydraulic tappets
Value Diameter: intake	in. (mm)	1.22 (31)
exhaust	in. (mm)	1.03 (26.2)
Valve Lift: intake	in. (mm)	0.3 (7.8)
exhaust	in. (mm)	0.3 (7.8)
Valve Timing: intake • opening		5° before T.D.C
• closing		51° after B.D.C
exhaust • opening		53° before B.D.C
• closing		15° after T.D.C.
Ignition System		Distributor-less
Firing Order		1-4-3-2
Fuel Tank Capacity	U.S. gal. (liters)	11.9 (45)
Fuel Pump		Electromagnetic
Lubrication System		Force-feed by trochoid gear pump
Oil Filter		Cartridge type
Engine Oil Capacity	U.S. gal. (liters)	0.95 (3.6)
Cooling System		Water-cooled
Water Pump		Centrifugal pump
Cooling Fan		5-blade electric
Coolant Capacity	U.S. gal. (liters)	1.25 (4.7)

DRIVETRAIN
Transmmision

Type		Five-speed manual
Gear Ratio	1st	3.136
	2nd	1.888
	3rd	1.330
	4th	1.000
	5th	0.814
	Reverse	3.758
Final Gear Ratio		4.300

Clutch

Type		Single dry plate diaphragm spring, hydraulically operated
Diameter	in. (mm)	7.9 (200)

CHASSIS
Front Suspension

Type		Independent by unequal-length upper-and-lower A-arms (double-wishbones), concentric coilsprings and shock absorbers, stabilizer-bar
Spring, Type		Coil
Rate at the Wheel	kgf/mm	1.6
Shock Absorber Type		Tubular double-acting, low-pressure gas-filled
Damping Rate at 0.1 m/s; rebound		60 kgf
Jounce		50 kgf
at 0.3 m/s; rebound		116 kgf
Jounce		80 kgf
Stabilizer, Type		Torsion bar
Diameter	in. (mm)	0.71 (18)

Weel Travel (unladen), Bound	in. (mm)	3.45 (87.8)
Rebound	in. (mm)	3.24 (82.2)
Wheel Geometry (unladen)		
camber degree		0°24′
caster degree		4°26′
toe-in	in. (mm)	0.04 (1)

Rear Suspension

Type		Independent by unequal-length upper-and-lower A-arms (double-wishbones), concentric coil springs and shock absorbers, stabilizer-bar
Springs, type		Coil
Rate at the Wheel	kgf/mm	1.4
Shock Absorber Type		Tubular double-acting, low-pressure gas-filled
Damping Rate at 0.1 m/s, Jounce	kgf	55
Rebound	kgf	25
at 0.3 m/s, Jounce	kgf	100
Rebound	kgf	40
Stabilizer, Type		Torsion bar
Diameter	in. (mm)	0.47 (12)
Wheel Travel (unladen), Jounce	in. (mm)	4.04 (102.5)
Rebound	in. (mm)	2.66 (67.5)
Weel Geomentry (unladen), camber degree		–0°43′
toe-in	in. (mm)	0.12 (3)

Steering

Type		Rack & Pinion (engine-speed-sensitive power assist available)
Overall Ratio		18:1 (15:1 with power assist)
Lock-to-Lock (turns)		3.3 (2.8 with power assist)
Turning Circle		
curb to curb	ft. (m)	30.3 (9.14)
wall to wall	ft. (m)	31.86 (9.71)
Steering Column		Collapsible

BRAKES

Type, front		Ventilated disc
rear		Solid disc
Front Disc diameter	in. (mm)	9.3 (236)
thickness	in. (mm)	0.71 (18)
brake pad area	in². (cm²)	5.83 (37.6)
Rear Disc diameter	in. (mm)	9.1 (231)
thickness	in. (mm)	0.35 (9)
brake pad area	in². (cm²)	4.1 (26.5)
Power Assist		8-in. vacuum booster
Parking Brakes		Mechanical on rear wheels

Tires and Wheels

Tires, front & rear		P185/60 R14 steel radial
Wheels, front & rear		5.5JJ×14 Styled steel or aluminum alloy

PERFORMANCE

Top Speed and Accleration		
Top Speed mph		116.8*
Standing Start 0-60 mph	seconds	8.6*
Maximum Lateral Accelerration	G	0.84*
Coefficient of Drag (CD)**		
soft top open		0.44
soft top closd		0.38

    * estimated on Mazda's internal test data
    ** measured in Mazda's wind tunnel testing laboratory

Fuel Economy (E.P.A estimates)		
City mode	mpg	25
Highway mode	mpg	35

1990 (1991 Model Year) J58W Series

Chronology:

August 1990

— Japanese "V Special" in British Racing Green exterior/Tan interior, leather seats and Nardi wood-rimmed steering wheel and shift knob. This color scheme model becomes the first U.S. "Special Edition" with Nardi shifter but not steering wheel; 4,000 units produced in the model year for America.

Mechanical changes and options:

— Optional 4-speed automatic transmission
— Optional removable hardtop in other colors
— Optional anti-lock brakes (ABS)

V Special in British Racing Green, Tan interior, leather seats and Nardi wood-rimmed steering wheel and wood shifter is added in Japan in August 1990. It becomes the first American Special Edition.

1991 (1992 Model Year) J58U Series

Chronology:

August 1991

— Japanese "J Limited" in Sunburst Yellow; 800 units. Also offered in the U.S., 1,500 units.

Mechanical changes and options:

— Optional ABS for Japanese models
— Optional removable hardtop

Eight hundred Sunburst Yellow J Limited models are offered in Japan in August 1991; this unique color scheme is offered in the U.S. in a limited run of 1,500 units.

1992 (1993 Model Year) J58X Series

Chronology:

September 1991

— "S Special" for Japan with firmer suspension, Bilstein shock absorbers, suspension tower bracebar and BBS forged aluminum wheels.
— U.S. "Limited Edition" in Black exterior/Red interior with Bilstein shocks, Nardi shifter, BBS wheels and aero pieces. This color scheme version becomes Japanese "S Limited" in January 1993; 1,000 units offered.

Mechanical changes and options:

— Driver-side SRS airbag option offered in Japan.
— Japanese models now fitted with side impact-bars within doors.

Japanese S Special with tuned suspension, Bilstein shock absorbers and BBS aluminum wheels. Rear suspension tower bracebar is added.

Japanese S Limited in Black exterior/Red interior combination; a limited run of 1,000 cars. This version is similar to the Limited Edition in the U.S.

1993 (1994 Model Year) J58L Series

Chronology:

First Update — The J58L 1800 Series

The J58L is the first major update of the MX-5, introduced in Japan in July 1993 and as the 1994 model elsewhere. In the J58L, the original B6-ZE 1.6-liter engine is replaced by the BP-ZE 1.8-liter unit.

Program manager Toshihiko Hirai took an early retirement toward the end of 1992 to pursue his academic career as professor of engineering at Oh-ita University. Deputy general manager Hiroshi Yamamoto of the then-First Vehicle Center filled-in at the position of program manager for the MX-5 for the update.

A change of the MX-5's heart — engine — had been deemed urgently necessary in the face of ever-tightening emission standards in its major markets, as well as safety requirements, the latter inevitably adding mass to the vehicle. Initially, Yamamoto's team considered a two-pronged approach, adding a 2.0-liter inline 4-cylinder option to the B6-ZE 1.6-liter engine which would obviously have to be updated. Yamamoto, however, reasoned that it would have stretched his already minimal resources to the limit. So he opted for a single engine, a mid-size one, thus the choice of the BP-ZE 1.8-liter unit.

While the BP-ZE shared its basic configuration with the B6-ZE — double overhead camshafts, 16 valves, electronic fuel injection and four cylinders — it obtained a cubic capacity of 1839 cc with 83-mm bore and 85-mm stroke. Hollow-cast twin overhead camshafts operate four valves per cylinder via inverted bucket tappets containing hydraulic lash adjusters in the aluminum cylinder head. Valves are inclined at an included angle of 50 degrees in a pentroof-shaped combustion chamber. Valve diameters are 33 mm for intake and 28 mm exhaust.

The BP-ZE engine has a sturdy cast iron, short-skirt block, and employs a highly rigid, forged steel crankshaft which is fully balanced with eight counterweights. The lower end adopts a cast aluminum oil pan, and an intricately shaped, pressed-steel vibration-reducing support plate (V.RSP) is inserted between the block and oil pan.

The type BP-ZE engine is rated at 128 bhp SAE net at 6,500 rpm and maximum torque of 110 lb-ft at 5,000 rpm on a 9.0:1 compression ratio in the U.S. specification Miata, 12 bhp and 10 lb-ft more than the 1600. The Japanese version puts out 130 ps JIS net and 157 Nm at the same rpm and compression ratio.

The bigger engine brought a welcome increase in the fuel tank capacity from the original 11.9 gallons U.S. (45 liters) to 12.7 gal. (48 liters).

As before, Mazda's own type-M 5-speed manual and N4A-EL 4-speed automatic transmissions were offered, combined with a taller 4.100:1 final-drive ratio (the 1600 had a 4.300:1). An optional new Torsen limited-slip differential was offered on manual transmission models.

Mazda also enlarged the brake rotors to match the engine's performance. In addition, the U.S. Miata got a redesigned instrument panel, incorporating a standard passenger-side SRS airbag. The Japanese series continued with the original right-hand-drive dashboard throughout the first-generation's life, SRS airbags still being non-mandated items in Japan.

1994 MIATA SPECIFICATIONS (U.S. Models)

Wheelbase	in.(mm)	89.2 (2,265)
Track, front	in.(mm)	55.5 (1,409)
rear	in.(mm)	56.2 (1,427)
Overall length	in.(mm)	155.4 (4,009)
width	in.(mm)	65.9 (1,675)
height	in.(mm)	48.2 (1,224)
Curb weight	lb (kg)	2,293 (1,042)
Engine		
Type BP		DOHC 16-valve inline 4
Bore x stroke	mm	83.0 x 85.0
Displacement	cc	1839
Compression ratio		9.0:1
Fuel system		Electronic, port fuel injection
Max power	bhp SAE net @ rpm	128 @ 6,500
Max torque	lb-ft SAE net @ rpm	110 @ 5,000
Transmission		
Type		5-speed manual gearbox
Gear ratios	1st	3.14
	2nd	1.89
	3rd	1.33
	4th	1.00
	5th	0.81
Final drive ratio		4.100:1
Optional transmission		4-speed automatic
Chassis		
Brake rotor dia, front, mm		255
rear, mm		251
Tires		P185/60HR14

Updated J58L gets the type BP-ZE 1.8-liter engine in July 1993.

— The U.S. "M Edition" is introduced during the model year. Christopher Lambert describes this edition in his comprehensive *A Guide for Miata in* America: "The introduction of the M Edition was marketing genius on the part of Mazda (North America). They did not have to adhere to automotive industry definitions of Limited Editions or Special Editions; they created their 'own' edition which became just as coveted by Miata enthusiasts."

December 1993
— Japanese counterpart to the American "genius" sprays 800 cars in Sunburst Yellow, naming it "J Limited II," fitted with Pirelli tires and high-power audio system.

Mechanical changes and options:
— BP-ZE 1.8-liter engine
— 4.100:1 final ratio
— Larger brakes
— Increased fuel tank capacity (48 liters)
— Passenger-side SRS airbag (U.S.)
— Torsen limited-slip differential
— Cross bracebar bridging the rear suspension top mounts, behind the seats

1994 (1995 Model Year) J58N Series

Chronology:
— U.S. "M Edition" includes 15-inch BBS wheels with P195/55VR15 high-performance tires, Tan vinyl soft top, Tan leather-trimmed lowback seats with embroidered Miata logo, Torsen limited-slip differential, leather Nardi shift knob and other accessories.
— U.S. "R Package" on manual transmission models; sports suspension, Bilstein shocks, front airdam, side skirts and rear spoiler, Torsen limited-slip differential.
— In certain countries in Europe, the 1600 is re-introduced as an entry model to receive favorable insurance rates for cars whose engine power is held under 90 ps (bhp). Essentially, the type B6-ZE is detuned to this output category.
— Japanese "RS Limited" in a batch of 500; with 15-inch BBS wheels shod with P195/55HR15 tires and Recaro bucket seats.

1995 J58N

Chronology:
January 1995
— Japanese "G Limited" in a batch of 1,500 units, still in the J58N series. This is essentially a luxury version in Starlight Mica Blue with matching Blue soft top, buckskin-like "Nu- buck" bucket seats and leather-wrapped Momo steering wheel and shifter.
February 1995
— Japanese "R Limited" in Starlight Mica Blue with Blue soft top/Red interior, 15-inch BBS wheels; 1,000 offered. This is also a version of the J58N series.

U.S. M Edition is added in 1993.

U.S. Models get redesigned instrument panel with dual SRS airbags; right-hand-drive models continue with the original instrument panel throughout the first generation.

M Edition's embroidered seats.

Japanese RS Limited, of which 500 units are offered in 1994.

1995 (1996 Model Year) J58P Series

Chronology:
The Final Version — Second Update
  The final series of the first-generation MX-5 Miata is the J58P which continues into 1997 Model Year with the same suffix. The series saw the second update, mainly in the BP-ZE engine which is fitted with a lightweight flywheel whose inertia mass has been reduced by 16 percent. Together with this modification, the engine control computer's capacity has been doubled, from the previous 8-bit to 16-bit, optimizing the

air/fuel ratio during high-speed operation.

Power output of the U.S. version is increased by 5 bhp to 133 bhp. The Japanese catalog quotes the same 130 ps (bhp), with a footnote that the modifications brought about a power increase "equivalent to 3 ps ."

The Japanese series are now fitted with a 4.300:1 final-drive ratio to exploit the improved engine's high-speed capability. The U.S. model continues with the 4.100:1 final-drive ratio.

The rear subframe cross bracebar is augmented by twin longitudinal rods extending forward in Japanese models to further improve chassis rigidity.

Mechanical changes and options:
— Rear subframe lateral bracebar for the U.S. series
— Rear subframe lateral and longitudinal brace rods on Japanese models

Second update in August 1995 included lightweight flywheel and more powerful engine management computer. Japanese models reverted to 4.30:1 final-drive ratio while U.S. versions continued with 4.10:1.

1996 (1997 Model Year) J58P Series

Chronology:
January 1996
— Japanese "VR Limited" based on the S Special; 1,500 units.
November 1996
— An aggregate production of 400,000 units is reached.
December 1996
— Japanese B2 Limited, 1,000 units, and R2 Limited in a batch of 500.

1987 (1998 Model Year) J58P Series

Chronology:
— Commemorative models for Japan and the U.S. for the final season of the First Generation.
— U.S. commemorative model is given the "STO" designation, which is short for "Still the One"; 3,000 units carry this most appropriate name selected from suggestions made by Mazda's American staff.
— Japan's own final version is given a less romantic "SR" designation and is produced in 700 copies.

Final Japanese model called SR Limited in a batch of 700 units; the U.S. Model gets a more appropriate designation STO — "Still the One."

Professor Toshihiko Hirai, father of the first generation MX-5 Miata, is "Still the One" program manager.

MX-5 MIATA/EUNES ROADSTER STATISTICS PRODUCTION, JAPANESE SALES, EXPORT

Calender Year	Production	Japanese Sales	Export Sales
1988	12	–	–
1989	45,266	9,307	34,021
1990	95,640	25,226	67,400
1991	63,434	22,594	40,729
1992	52,712	18,657	34,096
1993	44,743	16,789	27,909
1994	39,623	10,830	29,079
1995	31,886	7,178	27,648
1996	33,610	4,413	29,231
1997	24,618	3,331	21,698
Total	431,544	118,325	311,811

MAJOR EXPORT SALES

Calender Year	U.S.A.	Canada	Europe	Australia
1988	–	–	–	–
1989	23,052	2,827	–	621
1990	35,944	3,906	9,267	1,146
1991	31,240	2,956	14,050	746
1992	24,964	2,227	6,631	502
1993	20,588	1,501	4,824	453
1994	21,400	1,173	5,019	404
1995	20,174	934	7,176	196
1996	18,408	558	9,585	241
1997	16,791	562	10,119	201
Total	213,561	16,694	66,671	4,810

TOM MATANO'S STYLE

Tom Matano wears clothes of any color, as long as that color is black. "Black" Tom Matano is Executive Designer of Mazda's North American R&D arm based in Irvine, California. Matano's operation is far from that color. In fact, his studio produced such styling successes as the original MPV and the first-generation MX-5 Miata.

After penning their most successful creation, Matano and his designers did not rest on their laurels. "Past sports cars began life as roadsters, then there were variations ranging from club racers to speedsters, and coupes," says Matano. He followed this path faithfully, keeping the Miata design flame alive with several interesting and significant styling concept cars. Significant because with these design exercises, the California studio was preparing for the design of the second-generation Miata in competition with Mazda's three other design centers.

Club Racer — 1989 Chicago Auto Show Concept Model

When the Miata made its first public appearance at the Chicago Auto Show in February 1989, Matano's team already had a "club racer" concept car in the display. In less time than it takes to say, "Sports Car Club of America," Miatas began appearing on America's club racing scene. By far, mainly for its track-intended character, the car plays the most beautiful "music" through its straight-through exhaust pipe fitted with a token diffuser on its tip.

Mi-ari — Tribute to Ferrari, The Featured Marque of The 1994 Montery Historic Race

MRA built this car as its tribute to Enzo Ferrari's great creations on the occasion of the 1994 Monterey Historic Races, which hosted the prancing horses from Maranello as the featured marque. "Ferraris are magic," says Tom Matano. "There is something about the sight and sound of a Ferrari that stirs the soul of any sports car enthusiast."

The little speedster, affectionately dubbed "Mi-ari," was designed and built at Mazda R&D (MRA) in Irvine in 10 days during April, 1994. It features a cut-down windshield reminiscent of the 250 GT Testa Rossa of the late Fifties. Plexiglass vents on the hood and ducts on the front fenders recall the 250 GTO of the early Sixties, while the egg-crate grille is obviously a hallmark Ferrari cue.

The Mi-ari was shown to a small group of automotive journalists and friends, complete with an MRA staffer of appropriate physique (of Juan Manuel Fangio, or Froilan

Tom Matano and his designers were already at work before the official unveiling of the MX-5 Miata at the 1989 Chicago show, where this Club Racer version made its debut.

Club Racer's embroidered seats.

Gonzalez proportions) donning leather headgear.

If the Mi-ari's dedication to the prancing horses of Maranello was in its soul, then the car gave its body to MRA's next significant project, the M Speedster. Today, only the headrest/cowl piece of the car remains adorning the wall of an MRA executive office.

Hallmarks of racing Ferraris of the Fifties and Sixties are visible on the Mi-ari.

"Mi-ari" pays homage to the great prancing horses of Maranello — Ferraris at the 1984 Monterey Historic Automobile Races.

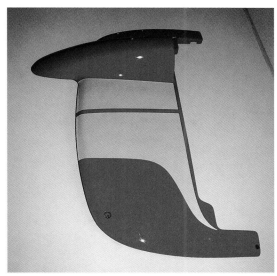

Only the hard tail/headrest remains of the Mi-ari, the rest of the body was resurrected in the M Speedster.

Photo by Bob Krueger

95

M Speedster — 1995 Concept Car

A speedster was the next passionate step taken by MRA in its Miata evolution. The speedster inherited its body from the Mi-ari which had been extensively restyled to impart a more muscular feel. Styling features include reshaped doors whose rear bottom edges sweep up like that of the RX-7 and extended rocker panels with pronounced lips to match the widened fenders.

Four projector-beam headlamps replace the standard round headlamps, lowering the lamp assembly height when it is raised. Additionally, two large driving lamps are placed in the more aggressive lower facia.

The Mi-ari's single driver-side headrest/cowl has been replaced by a twin-headrest/cowl with integrated compartments neatly housing matching helmets.

Two deeply contoured racing-type bucket seats replace the standard seats, complete with five-point racing safety belts. Seats, steering wheel, shift knob and handles are leather-covered with twin red stitches. Instrumentation is augmented by a compressor pressure gauge mounted on the driver-side A-pillar.

Apart from its outright flamboyant and racy looks, the M Speedster probed the possibility of a high-power Miata, one with an output in excess of 200 bhp. For this purpose, MRA employed Mazda's Lysholm compressor, the source of power and fuel efficiency of the Millenia S' Miller-cycle engine. In the M Speedster application, the Lysholm compressor is used purely as an ultra-high efficiency supercharger. The Lysholm compressor is unique in that it is a positive displacement compressor with internal compressing ability. It consists of a pair of helically lobed convex (male) and concave (female) screw-shaped rotors. The rotors pull fresh air in through the axial inlet port and push it toward the outlet port. In the process, the chamber created between the two rotors becomes sealed and its volume decreases as the trapped air is moved forward, thus compressing the air.

The supercharged BP-ZE 1.8-liter engine produces 200 bhp at 6,500 rpm and 165 lb-ft of torque at 5,500 rpm on a 9.0:1 compression ratio.

Speedster suspension modifications include progressive-rate springs, variable ride height, adjustable Koni shock absorbers, thicker anti-roll bars and P215/50ZR15 tires on 15 x 6-in. 5-spoke alloy wheels.

Muscular M Speedster.

Ready for the Mille Millia.

Quad projector headlamps are fitted, lowering raised lamp height.

Boost pressure gauge is mounted on the A-pillar.

Matching helmets are stored in the compartments under the twin headrests.

M Speedster is powered by a tuned BP-ZE engine boosted by a Lysholm positive-displacement compressor to a tune in excess of 200 bhp.

M Speedster's office sports racing bucket seats with five-point harnesses.

M Coupe completes Matano's trio—Club Racer, Speedster and Coupe in the first-generation Miata.

M Coupe has a perfectly usable trunk with spare wheel and battery buried underfloor.

Matano wanted to beat BMW and Mercedes, turning his roadster into a coupe, at least in spirit.

Final link between the first- and second-generation Miatas is this "Trunk Model." It is still based on the first-generation Miata, with unique outer panels.

Rear end is widened to create a usable trunk.

Trunk Model's proper trunk.

Face is unmistakably and friendly Miata, however, headlamps are now fixed.

M Coupe — 1996 New York Auto Show Concept Car

Tom Matano must have been anticipating the coupe versions that the Germans would be adding to their new roadsters, specifically BMW with the Z3 and Mercedes with the SLK. He wanted to "one-up" them, at least in the concept car arena, with the M Coupe.

As with the M Speedster, the coupe's stance has been slightly widened via wheels mounted with increased offset. The five-spoke, wide-rim wheels are shod with special Dunlop Sport 800 tires. The rear fender's ridge is more pronounced, accentuating the lower body's flowing profile. Door and rocker panel shapes are similar to the M Speedster's, suggesting design cues that would be reflected in the California studio's proposal for the new MX-5.

The roof line, exquisitely formed in fiberglass by MRA's craftsmen, has subtle RX-7-like double-bubbles. By moving the spare wheel to underneath the body and relocating the battery deeper, Matano's designers were able to significantly increase trunk room versus the roadster. And the shelf behind the seats can take some small luggage items, held by a folding aluminum rack.

Mechanically, the M Coupe is stock Miata with a 133-bhp, 1.8-liter engine.

Trunk Model — Prelude To The Next Generation

This is a rare non-runner among Matano's collection of first-generation Miata concept models. It is still based on an off-the-shelf, first-generation Miata. Its mission was not to "look" or "go" faster, but rather to incorporate one important improvement fervently wished for by many a Miata owner: a larger trunk, thus the moniker "Trunk Model."

The car's rear end is pushed out a few inches, with sheet metal appropriately shaped to cover the expansion. The spare and battery are relocated, *á la* M Coupe, and *voilà*, a proper trunk-shaped trunk of significantly increased volume appears. In the process of the conversion, Tom Matano and his designers incorporated all the design cues they considered appropriate for a future roadster. The "Trunk Model" thus bears uncanny resemblance to the second-generation MX-5, and the project was undertaken before the official kick-off of the competition among Mazda's four studios. The Trunk Model is indeed the link between the first- and second-generation Miatas.

One side of the Trunk Model, has a curved door like the M Speedster and Coupe.

The other side retains the original door.

Progression of Irvine's Miata theme is seen in these profiles

Club Racer.

M Speedster.

M Coupe.

Miata Evolution.

Trnk Model.

Honey, I shrunk my Miata! Tom Matano's human-powered car. The pedal car is built around a sturdy tubular steel frame on which the fiberglass body is mounted.

1999

1999 MX-5 Miata with aero pieces.

The roadster bridging two worlds? Wu-Huang Chin's rendering of the Miata-rado, paying homage to the retiring GM vice president — Design, Chuck Jordan. This is a father-and-son car, combining the unmistakable styling cues from Chuck's tail-finned Eldorado and Mark Jordan's Miata.

California gang: design team of Mazda North American Operations R&D center.
From left: Truman Pollard, Tom Martinez, Ken Seward, Hideki Suzuki, Thom Nishida, Mark Jordan, Akira Ide, Wu-Huang Chin, Gary Vasquez, Tom Matano, Tom Monarch and Debby Dodge. (Two who were not present are Ed Blandford and Gary Gastmyer.)

THE M2 EXPERIMENT

"The monstrous new city hall in metropolitan Tokyo won't have to wait long before it is challenged by another architectural oddity, Mazda's new M2 headquarters," wrote author Jack Yamaguchi in *Road & Track's* July 1991, issue. "Although much smaller in scale, the Mazda building is, nevertheless, as scary as the city hall — Dracula's mansion, Trump Tower and Darth Vader's evil star rolled into one."

R&T's art director Richard Baron was kinder in his description: "It reminded me of the movie *Brazil,*" Baron said.

To defend the honor of the inspirational architect Kengo Kuma, the design was to transcend the antagonism between industry and people, being functional, sleek and luxurious, and also softer and more human.

The residents of the house of M2, a wholly owned subsidiary of Mazda Motor Corporation, had noble intention. They were charged with keeping in touch with the elusive needs and desires of Japan's youthful drivers, and to turn out innovative niche-mobiles based on volume-production Mazda models. The site was ideally suited: the Setagaya section of Tokyo facing the busy stretch of the Loop Road 8 where the fashionable set dwelled and congregated and neat cars gathered.

Heading the M2 operation was Masakatsu Kato, father of the

original lightweight sports car project, the P729/V705, as well as creator of several Mazda concept vehicles. His lieutenant and technical director was Hirotaka Tachibana, the development engineer responsible for the superb dynamics of the second-generation RX-7 and the original MX-5 Miata.

By far the most popular model the M2 converted was the roadster.

M2 1001 — November 1991, Limited Production

Tachibana, formerly senior manager of the Vehicle Research and Testing Department, is an accomplished development engineer, enthusiast and a superb driver. Given free rein at M2, Tachibana set out to accomplish what he had left undone in Hiroshima: Develop and build his ideal MX-5, unfettered by the productivity and cost constraints imposed on series production automobiles, with the full support and dedication of a small design and development team of young engineers created within Mazda's product development division in Hiroshima. Actual conversion and tuning was carried out by Mazda Sangyo, a Hiroshima-based subsidiary engineering company, which was also commissioned to build a batch of 300 cars to be sold through the M2.

For all intents and purposes it was a cost-no-object project; whatever yen spent on development would be passed along to the buyer. Tachibana's attitude was, "Take it or leave it."

The M2 "1001" was announced in November 1991, at 3.4 million yen (more than $26,000), almost twice the base price of the Eunos Roadster, the Japanese moniker for the MX-5. Two hundred examples were quickly whisked away by willing takers, and for the final 100, a lottery decided who would be the lucky owners.

The B6-ZE engine's compression was raised to 10.57:1 by a set of special pistons. High-lift camshafts, polished ports and a freer exhaust system added 14 bhp, hiking the output to 130 bhp at 6,500 rpm and now requiring premium-grade unleaded fuel. Torque was increased throughout the engine's entire rev range, peaking at 110 lb-ft (148 Nm) at 5,500 rpm.

M2 1001 was a very serious cost-no-object attempt at an ideal LWS (light-weight sports car) by Mazda's own skunkworks in Tokyo.

Roll-over bar added to the body's stiffness.

Three-spoke, polished alloy steering wheel, brushed aluminum shift gate plate and brightwork around the meters and gauges.

Type B6-ZE 1.6-liter engine was tweaked with high-compression pistons, high-lift camshafts and polished headers, and put out an additional 14 bhp.

A more expensive Torsen limited-slip differential replaced the original viscous type. An arduous track test revealed that the car's improved performance tended to overheat the final drive, so an aluminum duct was added, which lowered temperature by as much as 20 degrees Celsius.

The suspension featured firmer springs and specifically tuned shock absorbers, and Tachibana persuaded Dunlop to tool 300 sets of special 195/50VR15 tires to replace the original car's 185/60R14s.

The exterior of the 1001 was fitted with an oversize front airdam integrating a pair of powerful fog lamps, rear spoiler, unique rear-view mirrors and a racing-type fuel filler cap. Under the hood was a front suspension tower reinforcing cross bar, and inside, the Boy Racer image was accentuated by a hefty roll-over loop.

The cockpit featured proper bucket seats, a leather-wrapped 3-spoke steering wheel with brushed-chrome accents and a matching brushed-Chrome shift knob.

The 1001 was followed by the 1002, announced in October 1992, which was less exorbitant but still quite comprehensively equipped, carrying a price tag of 3 million yen. A limited run of 300 cars were produced.

M2 1006 — "Cobraster" V6-powered Concept Car

By far the wildest Tachibana creation was the 1006 "Cobraster," as it was referred to by Mazda's insiders in deference to the Ford/Shelby creation of the Sixties. This widened MX-5 was powered by a quad-cam, 24-valve V6 engine from the 929 sedan. The car featured a wider track and RX-7 rear suspension. Tachibana's intention was to produce a limited number of this mini terror using a 2.5-liter version of the V6, but the project went no further than building two cars, one for show and the other for unsanctioned "go."

M2 1006, powered by the 929's quad-camshaft, 24-valve V6, is called "Cobraster" by Mazda's insiders.

M2 1008 — M2's Coupe Concept

Another one-off project, this was M2's idea of a coupe derivative of the original theme. Its styling was a more radical departure than the California M Coupe which remained true to the Miata principle. The 1008, nevertheless, had its own cheeky charm highlighted by its Italian cutoff tail.

M2 1028 — February 1994, M2's Final Limited Production Model

The 1028 is the final "production" roadster offered by the M2, again in a batch of 300 cars, this time with a price of 2.8 million yen a copy. This was essentially a less lavishly equipped, racer-like (M2 called it "street-competition," another way of saying Miata stop-light grand prix) version with an aluminum rollcage attached to the body at ten points, significantly contributing to the latter's stiffness. It came with a special lightweight hardtop as standard equipment. The tuned BP-ZE 1.8-liter engine yielded 10 bhp over the stock unit, now putting out 140 bhp at 6,500 rpm on a higher 10.6:1 compression ratio.

By then, former design boss Shigenori Fukuda had taken over the M2. He reminisces, "Actually, I was there to wrap up the operation, which was becoming too expensive for the company to maintain in the aftermath of Japan's burst Bubble economy and Mazda's waning fortunes."

Wide track suggests an RX-7 rear suspension.

Two cars were built, one for show and the other for go.

1006's vicious bite was infected by the quad-cam, 24-valve V6.

The Setagaya gang had the same idea as Irvine's covert team, turning the roadster into a coupe, the M2 1008.

1008 has an Italianesque cut-off tail.

MAZDASPEED CREATIONS

Mazdaspeed is a Tokyo-based subsidiary of Mazda Motor Corporation, specializing in supplying go-faster conversions and components for various Mazda products. Its most notable achievements are its sports racing car activities during the Eighties and early Nineties.

Mazdaspeed challenged the world's most gruelling test of man and machine, the classic 24-hour endurance race for sports cars at Le Mans in 1979 with the type 252i, a highly modified first-generation RX-7. It failed to make the grid, lacking necessary speed. Le Mans fever consumed Mazdaspeed which continued its efforts with total obsession. Its best showing in the Eighties was 7th overall in the 1989 race with one of the quad-rotor 767B cars.

By then the rotary's days on the race track were numbered in view of the FIA's proposal which would limit future Le Mans race cars to using naturally aspirated piston engines with a maximum displacement of 3.5 liters (which was to be rescinded). Mazda's management, acutely aware of the imminent danger, decided to overhaul and strengthen the company's racing activities by appointing Takaharu "Koby" Kobayakawa, the program manager for the RX-7, to the position of *de facto* racing director of the total Mazda efforts, including Mazdaspeed, in 1990. Kobayakawa's newly recruited team of designers and engineers included Takao Kijima, chassis designer and lieutenant for development of the third-generation RX-7. Kijima applied his analytical skills to the 787 racer which was designed by Britain's Nigel Stroud. The chassis was reinforced and strengthened on Kijima's recommendation, progressing to the B specifications. Takao Kijima is the program manager for the new MX-5 Miata.

The 787B, driven by Johnny Herbert, Volker Weidler and Bertrand Gachot, won the 1991 Le Mans 24-hour endurance race outright — the first ever by a Japanese marque. Mazdaspeed was an important and integral part of Mazda's endeavor to achieve this victory.

Mazdaspeed offers a variety of interesting and effective performance parts and conversions for the roadster.

Bolt-on Eaton Supercharger

Mazdaspeed adapted the Eaton supercharger to the roadster's engines, first on the B6-ZE 1.6-liter unit and later the BP-ZE 1.8-liter. The bolt-on supercharger kit hikes these engine's outputs to 170 bhp and 180 bhp at 7,200 rpm, respectively. The installation costs 450,000 yen, about $3,460 (at $1-to-130-yen exchange rate; the rate has been roller-coasting between an uncomfortably high value of 80 yen to a dollar,

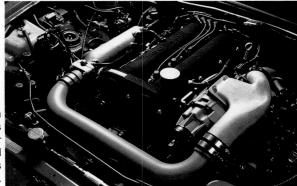

Mazdaspeed's bolt-on Eaton supercharger hikes the 1.6- and 1.8-liter engines up to 170 bhp and 180 bhp, respectively. This is the 1.8 installation.

to an equally discomforting low of 140, so please apply whatever is ongoing).

Touring B-Spec NA

Mazdaspeed also offers performance conversions retaining the engines' natural aspiration (NA). High-compression pistons, high-lift camshafts, lightweight flywheel, specific electronic control unit, and freer exhaust system are included in the package. Stage I conversion increases the 1.6-liter engine's power to 130 bhp and the 1.8's to 145 bhp. Hotter Stage II increases outputs to 144 bhp and 170 bhp, respectively. Prices range between 350,000 and 870,000 yen.

C-Spec

Mazdaspeed's ultimate conversion of the first-generation is the C-Spec, introduced a mere month before the new MX-5 was officially launched in Japan. The C-Spec is a defiant piece of styling which has few hints of the original car. It features a single-piece hood/bumper/facia with fixed headlamps under acryl covers, widened fenders (which put the car out of the Japanese small car category, exceeding the maximum 1.7-meter width,) unique taillamps and retractable rear wing, all made of fiber-reinforced plastic, and all for the sake of superior aerodynamics.

The car measures 4,135 mm long, 1,750 mm wide and 1,215 mm tall and weighs 1,010 kg.

The engine is called BP-ZE Modified, and is a bored and stroked version of the 1.8 unit, with 84.5 mm bore and 89.0 mm stroke, displacing 1995 cc. The engine is fitted with a unique forged steel crankshaft, high-compression pistons, special camshafts of long valve opening duration and higher lift (10.5 mm), polished ports, straight intake manifold with quad-throttle valves, and 4-into-2-into-1 exhaust manifold. The engine produces 200 bhp at 7,400 rpm and 147 lb-ft torque (201 Nm) at 5,000 rpm.

The chassis is suitably tuned to handle increased performance, and includes manually adjustable shock absorbers with vehicle height adjustment ability, firmer springs, 23-mm diameter solid stabilizer bars, front and rear aluminum suspension-tower bracebars, friction-plate-type limited-slip differential and fat Dunlop 205/45R16 tires on 16 x 8J three-spoke alloy wheels.

Modifications are so extensive that the C-Spec no longer has the factory warranty, but is covered by Mazdaspeed's equal if not superior support. The base C-Spec is priced at 4.35 million, about $33,500 (at $1=130 yen rate), and the Special version with ivory/tan interior and full complement of comfort and entertainment equipment costs an additional million.

Aero-kit II offered by Mazdaspeed.

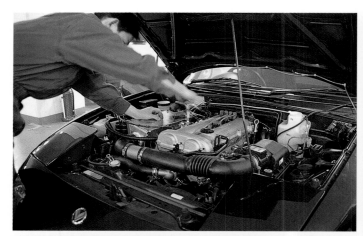

C-Spec is Mazdaspeed's final and ultimate street-legal conversion of the first-generation roadster. Its engine is enlarged to a full 2.0 liters and tuned to produce 200 bhp at 7,400 rpm.

MIATA RACING IN AMERICA

Mazda has a long and honored corporate involvement in racing, including a win at the prestigious Le Mans 24-Hour Endurance Race in 1991. Here in America, the RX-7 has been a dominating force in racing since the first rotary-powered sports car took to the track in February, 1979 in the Daytona 24-Hour Endurance race. Two factory-prepared RX-7s were entered in the GTU category and the lucky #7 entry took the GTU win, finishing 5th overall. From 1980 through 1989, Mazda won the IMSA GTU championship nine out of the 10 years.

RX-7s also competed and won in the GTO category, capturing the drivers' and manufacturers' championships in 1991. Mazda rotaries have also found considerable success in prototype racing, both in the Camel Lights under 3-liter category and in the top-of-the-class GTP category.

European sports cars, which found their way to this country following World War II, provided the catalyst for the creation of the Sports Car Club of America. And it wasn't long before these cars were making their "marque" on races tracks that sprung up all around the country beginning in the late 1940s.

It was obvious from our first brief review of the Miata's specifications that it would have a natural affinity for a race track. And like the MGs, Triumphs, Austin-Healeys, Porsches, Alfas and Jaguars that preceded it, it wasn't long before the Miata was proving itself a worthy adversary in the rigors of competition.

When the Miata Club of America was first formed, brothers Duane and Randy Simpson were picked to lead the Club's competition efforts. Under the title Simpson Brothers Racing, the Simpson duo spearheaded the Miata's racing efforts, running selected professional and national road racing and SCCA Solo events. The knowledge and experience the Simpsons gained modifying Miatas for these various events was passed along to other Miata competitors. After two seasons, the Simpsons moved over to let other MX5 enthusiasts carry on the battle.

The Miata's first race was the September, 1989, Escort Endurance Series 9-hour event at Road Atlanta. Because the Escort Series required that the car be basically stock, many of the components that would normally be removed or highly modified had to be left in place. However, as anyone who has raced showroom stock racing can attest to, just because the rules require a relatively unmodified vehicle, that doesn't make the racing preparation task any easier. In fact, it makes it much more difficult and time consuming.

For its first race the Simpsons removed the Miata's air conditioning system, the air bag and the catalytic converter and added a late-model RX-7 steering wheel and a straight pipe fitted with a Walker Dynomax muffler. The rollcage proved to be a bit of an engineering feat. Because the Simpsons wanted the car to be legal for different classes, the bars running forward from the main rollover hoop could not go through the dash. That required a design that interfered with convenient entry and exit, a significant annoyance during an endurance race because it lengthened the time needed for driver changes. The only other changes from stock that the rules allowed were the driver's seat, shock absorbers, brake pads, wheels and tires.

The Miata's major competition came from the Honda CRX Si, but the Volkswagen GTi 16v, Peugeot 505 Turbo, Chevrolet Beretta and Suzuki Swift were also formidable competition. In that first event the Miata finished 25th out of 41 cars. Duane Simpson felt this was a respectable showing considering the

Photo by B. Klingler

field included a bunch of much faster Camaros, Mustangs and Nissan 300ZX Turbos.

Although there are classes in professional racing that include the Miata, it's in amateur SCCA racing where the Miata has enjoyed the most success. Beginning in 1994 and continuing for the next two years, Miatas with the 1.6-liter engine took home Showroom Stock (SS) C victories at the SCCA Valvoline Runoffs National Championships.

Following a drought of two years, the Miata charged back to another Showroom Stock National title in 1997, this time in Class B with the 1.8-liter R model.

In Production Class racing almost all bets are off. What this means is that the car must retain certain selected specs — general appearance, basic engine block, etc. — but most of the internal engine components including the crank, pistons, rods and valves can be changed as long as they remain within SCCA guidelines. For example, boring and/or stroking the engine to 2.5-liters or adding a turbocharger would get you a front row seat at the NHRA Funny Car Nationals, but a quick "boot" at any SCCA-sanctioned event. But in other ways the car can be stripped, gutted, lowered and widened. In other words, an SCCA Production Class Miata would not be a street legal automobile. Running in E Production, Miatas have captured two National Championship titles, the first in 1994 and the most recent in 1997. Leading up to those two championships are 25 SCCA National wins, between the years 1994-1997.

Early Miatas are now old enough to qualify for SCCA Improved Touring racing. IT, as it is often called, is the place where cars that are more highly modified than Showroom Stock rules allow, but which aren't "pure" race cars in the sense of the various National and Regional Production Classes, can find a home. Improved Touring caters to older models, so the entry price is lower than for SS or Production racing. And allowable modifications tend toward those that make the car faster but not horribly expensive to build or maintain. Racing an IT car is one of the best ways to get started in serious track

competition.

If you'd like to get a taste of racing before making an all-out commitment to the sport, then autocrossing is the place to start. If you're not familiar with autocross, imagine a large parking lot with a tight, twisty road marked with those familiar orange cones used by highway departments to close lanes or otherwise divert traffic. The idea is to drive the course as quickly as possible without knocking over any cones. The fastest time wins and because fast time is relative, there are different classes for different types of cars and for differing levels of modification, ranging from totally stock to cars that have to be towed to events because they aren't street legal. Autocrossing is a great way to develop your driving skills because of the lessons it teaches in car control when driving at the limit. And if you make a mistake, the worst that usually happens is several seconds added to your time for knocking over cones and a face that is slightly red from embarrassment.

Many Miata Clubs organize low-key autocross events. For more serious competitors there are SCCA Solo II and ProSolo2 autocrosses which lead to National Championships not unlike the National road racing Runoffs. Between 1993 and 1997 Miatas have scored a total of 20 National Championship victories in a variety of different classes. Last year Miatas dominated Solo II autocrossing, even after being moved from Class C to the faster Class B.

What does 1998 have in store for the new 1999 Miata? Most sanctioning bodies haven't classified the new Miata yet. The Miata won SSC in 1997 and the new car should be a little faster. But fast enough to be moved up to Showroom Stock A where it would have to go head-to-head and fender-to-fender against 6-cylinder BMW 328s and VW Corrados? That doesn't seem likely, so look for the 1999 Miata to remain in SSB.

The same sort of scenario is also being played out in Solo racing where the new Miata could be moved up to the A Stock ranks.

Last year the Miata ran the SportsCar Speedvision Cup as a

Photo by Gordon L. Jolley

Photo by Mark Weber

Compact against the likes of the Honda del Sol, Dodge/Plymouth Neon and the Nissan Sentra SE-R. The Miata had to rely upon its superior brakes and handling because it had the least horsepower in its class. SportsCar eventually allowed the car a few additional modifications to bring it into parity with its competitors. This helped the Protomotive Team capture the Miata's first professional win.

The 1999 model, thanks to a slight increase in power, should prove to have an advantage in pro racing trim for 1998. But as we go to press, all the rules haven't been set in stone (will they ever?) and all the dust hasn't settled, so we'll just have to consult our ouija boards to figure out exactly what the Miata's prospects are for racing success during 1998.

HISTORY OF MAZDA MIATA VICTORIES IN SCCA COMPETITION

SCCA Valvoline Runoffs National Championship Victories

E Production	1997, 1994
Showroom Stock B (Miata R)	1997
Showroom Stock C (Miata)	1994, 1993, 1992

Club Racing National Wins by Year

1997	10 EP, 49 SSB, 3 SSC
1996	7 EP, 39 SSB, 11 SSC
1995	6 EP, 18 SSB, 32 SSC
1994*	2 EP, 50 SSC
1993*	73 SSC (out of 73)
1992*	61 SSC
1991*	45 SSC

Solo II National Championship Victories

B Stock**	1997
B Stock Ladies**	1997
C Stock	1996, 1995, 1994
C Stock Ladies	1996, 1995, 1994, 1993
C Street Prepared	1997
C Stock Prepared Ladies	1997, 1996

ProSolo2 National Championships

B Stock*	1997
C Stock (Stock 3)	1996, 1995, 1994
Overall	
Ladies	1996
Club	1997, 1996
Ladies Club	1996

*Club Racing National Wins by marque: may include wins by the Mazda Protegé and other Mazda vehicles during 1991-1994.

**The Miata was moved to B Stock in Solo II and ProSolo2 in 1997 as part of a Stock class restructuring.

Chart provided courtesy of Richard James, Senior Editor, *SportsCar,* the official publication of the SCCA.

MIATA CLUB OF AMERICA

Early last January, Jack Gerken, a long-time friend and one of the true automotive public relations professionals, and I were cruising up the 405 freeway linking Orange County and Los Angeles. We were on our way to the LA Convention Center for "press day," Actuallys, its two days of non-stop press conferences prior to the official public opening of the Los Angeles Auto Show, during which the various auto companies displaying product get an opportunity to do a "show and tell" for the local automotive media.

We were traveling through the Gardena area when I turned to Jack and said, "Did you notice all the Miatas? We've probably passed a dozen of them. And there's another, and another and another…" By the time we got tired of saying "and another," we'd probably counted 50 Miatas. Being the middle of the week, I figured they couldn't be traveling to a weekend Miata club event or a race someplace North.

"Maybe they're going to the auto show," I casually said to Jack as we turned off the 405 and headed up the Harbor Freeway. But no, they continued their journey up the 405 and they were soon forgotten in the mess of morning rush hour traffic we encountered as we got closer and closer to the downtown LA area.

Surprise! As we turned into the underground parking garage at the Convention Center, guess what we ran into (figuratively, not literally)? All those Miatas. Today was "show time," the day and the auto show Mazda had chosen to unveil the new 1999 Miata to the assembled enthusiast press.

During my years in this business, I have met numerous members of marque clubs. But it wasn't until Jack Yamaguchi invited me to partner with him in the creation of this book that I came to a realization and an appreciation of the important role the Miata Club of America has played in spreading the Miata gospel, not just in America, but around the world.

Even before the launch of the Miata in 1989, Mazda had more than 60 unsolicited proposals for creation of a formal Miata club, which would include a Miata publication, member and membership services, a racing division, chapter support service and an international club division. Ultimately, Norman Garrett, one of the original Miata design engineers, Vince Tidwell, formerly an officer of the BMW Club, and Barbara Beach of MediaSource were selected as the team to build what would become The Miata Club of America.

Today, the club has grown to more than 80 local chapters spread throughout the U.S. and Canada, plus around the world in Germany, Italy, Australia, Japan, the Philippines and South Africa, to name but a few. Since the club was officially born on November, 1, 1987, more than 65,000 people have signed on to join the MCA, the only Miata club officially recognized by the factory.

Miata Magazine is the Club's official publication. Written expressly for Miata aficionados, it is a professionally crafted, well written 100-page, bi-monthly magazine containing Miata news and background, coming events, driving techniques, service tips from the pros, money-saving Miata advice, Miata modifications and member correspondence.

The Club has held national events in such places as Laguna Seca in conjunction with the annual Historic Car Races and in Irvine, California, home of Mazda's R & D Center and birthplace of the Miata. Regionally, those 80 plus local clubs provide a variety of regional events and social activities for Miataphiles worldwide.

If you are interested in joining the MCA, write to MCA Memberships, Box 920428, Norcross, GA 30010 or call 770 642-4482. Dues are $29 per year. The club also has a website: **www.miatas.net**

ROADSTER CLUB OF JAPAN

The Roadster Club of Japan (RCOJ) was established in 1996 as a coordinating body of Japan's regional and local clubs. The name "Roadster" comes from the car's Japanese name, the Eunos Roadster (affectionately shortend to "ER"). With the integration of Eunos dealers into the Mazda dealer network, this has been changed to Mazda Roadster for the new model.

Masanori Mizuochi, representative of the RCOJ and formerly with Mazda and M2, reports that the membership reached 1,120 as of March 1998. The RCOJ publishes its quarterly magazine *Roadster Club Magazine* (text is in Japanese).

The participating clubs hold various events including autocrosses. The RCOJ maintains active contact with the MX-5 clubs in other countries.

Chapter

4

THEN THERE WERE MORE

MIATA RIVALS

Isn't it interesting that the more things change, the more they remain the same? Take sports cars for instance. Within the past few years we've witnessed the demise of Nissan's 300ZX, Mazda's RX-7 and Porsche's 968. (The RX-7, however, is very much alive in its home country where the marque is strongly identified with the rotary engine.) Toyota's super Supra and Mitsubishi's techno-wiz 3000GT have survived the auditor's ax, but both are limited-volume specialty cars which, like their fallen brethren, have watched their fortunes drop, victims of changing life styles and rampant SUV-ism.

But while all this was occurring, behind the scenes other forces were at work, recreating a class of sports car that had all but disappeared, except for a class of one, from the face of America.

That "one," of course, is the Mazda Miata. Now it has three compatriots in charm, from one of the least likely places, Germany, vying for the emotions and the dollars of American motorists. In Europe, the two old guards of the sports car movement, Great Britain and Italy, have rejoined the battle, seeking euro and yen, but unfortunately not dollars, because they have chosen not to compete in the land where they enjoyed their greatest sports car successes.

Welcome to the rebirth of the classic roadster! Three of Germany's major players — BMW, Mercedes-Benz and Porsche — have joined the fray in the form of the Z3, SLK and the Boxster, respectively. Also making sports car noises these days are Rover of Britain with the MGF and Italy's auto giant Fiat with the Barchetta. So for the first time in half a dozen years, the Miata has some serious competitors, marking "their" territory and making claim to the title "Best of the Best."

BMW Z3

This roadster has a total Southern connection stretching across two continents. Bred in Southern Germany, Bavaria to be precise, and built in South Carolina (yes, the one more famous for door-banging NASCAR racing than effete sporty cars), the Z3 has more than a passing familiarity with the Miata. Both are front-engine, rear-drive automobiles with handsome muscular styling, simple-to-stow-and-erect manually operated tops, 2-liter (okay, okay, close to 2-liters) inline 4-cylinder

engines and standard 5-speed manual transmissions. Dimensionally, they are also comparable, but the Z3 rides on a substantially longer — by 7.1 inches — wheelbase, which accounts for some significant differences between the Miata and the Z3 when it comes to such things as handling and ride. And unlike the Miata, which is offered only one way, with the Z3 you get a choice of engine under the hood — a 2.8-liter inline-6 as well as the base 1.9-liter 4-banger — a soon-to-arrive "M" version of the six which will pump out 240 bhp, and two different body styles, roadster and (in the near future) a fixed-head coupe. "Fixed-head" refers to the fact that the Z3's hardtop can't be removed as it can be with the Miata's removeable hardtop.

Like classic roadsters of yore, some of the Z3's components have been selected from the corporate parts bins of higher-volume sedan models. There are obvious efficiencies in both design and cost to be achieved by this approach. In the case of

the Z3, the engine and suspension were all derived from the 3-Series. The 4-cylinder engine is shared with the 318ti Coupe as are the front MacPherson strut suspension and the semi-trailing arms used at the rear. Why not use the multi-link rear suspension found in the other 3-Series models? The semi-trailing arms allow for better packaging — a fairly reasonable trunk — which would have been impossible with the multi-link design.

The 2.8-liter inline-6 is in the Z3 represents BMW's first U.S. use of the aluminum-block six, which is lighter than the cast iron block by more than 50 lb. It's rated at 189 bhp and includes double-overhead cams, direct-port fuel injection, 4-valves per cylinder, BMW's own engine management system and a variable-cam-adjustment system called VANOS.

As you'd expect, the Z3 2.8 is much more than just a bigger engine. This model also includes a heavy-duty Getrag 5-speed manual gearbox, reinforced rear suspension with a 2.5-inch wider track, a standard limited-slip differential (not available with the 1.9), revised suspension geometry and calibration and bigger brakes. Visually, the 2.8 is distinguished by wider rear fenders, special wheels and a unique front bumper and spoiler.

Like the Miata, the Z3 cockpit is strictly for two with minimal room behind the seats. While the dual cupholders are a Nineties convenience, the cockpit's dual-cowl styling is reminiscent of old English roadsters.

On the road the Z3 feels more like a roadster than it does a sports car. And this is true of both models. That's not to imply they aren't sporty. *Au contraire.* However, neither provokes the same sort of Michael Andretti adrenaline rush that I experience behind the wheel of a Miata. For example, around corners there is an uncharacteristically large amount of body roll for a sports car. Yet the handling balance is delightful once you acclimate to the body roll. The brakes in both models are strong and powerful and the steering provides very good feel and feedback. But the combination of steering and tires make the Z3 sensitive to pavement irregularities of the type encountered on some Southern California grooved freeways.

Thanks to its relatively long wheelbase, there is a sedan-like quality to the Z3's ride. This, in combination with its greater weight — around 400-500 lb more than a Miata — add up to a surprisingly plush ride for a relatively small car.

While the 1.9-liter provides the Z3 with performance on a par with the Miata, subjectively, the Mazda feels quicker and more responsive. Credit this to the Miata's lovely 5-speed gearbox and perfectly spaced gears. The 1.9 also would benefit from an exhaust note that sounds like it belongs to a sports car. This one is merely raspy.

The 2.8-liter six's added power and torque endow the Z3 with wonderful flexibility and silky, smooth acceleration. This is the sort of power that makes for effortless around-town performance and quiet cruising. It's the ability to stick the shift lever in 5th gear and not worry about the engine falling off the torque curve regardless of how low the revs drop. But this is not necessarily sports car performance because it doesn't involve you with the driving the way I believe a sports car should.

At a base price of $29,995 ($36,470 for the Z3 2.8) the Z3 is nearly $10,000 more expensive than an entry-level Miata. And certainly it offers a higher level of standard equipment, including power windows, door locks and seats, cruise control and All Season Traction (AST). But in some ways the level of quality doesn't match the higher price tag. For instance, with the top up, the Z3 is much noisier because of wind noise. Squeaks and rattles are much more noticeable in the Z3 and the Miata also has a more solid structure.

For 1998, all Z3s get a standard rollover bar. And, incredibly, a power top is being offered. This one is tough to figure. When you already offer one of the world's simplest-to-operate manual convertible tops, why complicate people's lives (and their wallets) with a power option? This is one of the Miata's real attractions. Mazda continues to focus its attention on things that add to a sports car's intrinsic driving pleasure and away from features that simply increase complexity and cost.

SPECIFICATIONS

ENGINE

Z3 1.9

Type	dohc 16-valve inline-4
Displacement, cc	1895
Compression ratio	10.0:1
Horsepower, bhp (kW) SAE net @ rpm	138 (102) @ 6,000
Torque, lb-ft (Nm) SAE net @ rpm	133 (180) @ 4,300

Z3 2.8

Type	24-valve inline-6
Displacement, cc	2793
Compression ratio	10.2:1
Horsepower, bhp (kW) SAE net @ rpm	189 (140) @ 5,300
Torque, lb-ft (Nm) SAE net @ rpm	203 (274) @ 3,950

Z3 M

Type	dohc 24-valve inline-6
Displacement, cc	3152
Compression ratio	10.5:1
Horsepower, bhp (kW) SAE net @ rpm	240 (178) @ 6,000
Torque, lb-ft (Nm) SAE net @ rpm	236 (318) @ 3,800

DRIVETRAIN

Transmission	5-speed manual (optional 4-speed automatic)
Final-drive ratio, 1.9; 2.8; M	3.45:1; 3.15:1; 3.23:1

CHASSIS & BODY

Layout	front engine/rear drive
Suspension, front/rear	MacPherson struts, lower L-arms, coil springs, tube shocks (gas-charged twin-tube with 2.8 and M), anti-roll bar/semi-trailing arms, coil springs, tube shocks (gas-charged twin-tube with 2.8 and M), anti-roll bar
Steering	rack & pinion, power assist
Turns, lock to lock, 1.9; 2.8; M	2.9; 2.7; 3.2
Brakes, front/rear	solid discs (vented with 2.8 and M)/solid discs (vented discs with M)
Wheels, 1.9; 2.8; M	16 x 7J front, 17 x 8.5J rear; 17 x 7.5J front, 17 x 8.5J rear; 17 x 7.5J front, 17 x 9J rear
Tires, 1.9; 2.8; M	225/50ZR16 front, 245/40ZR17 rear; 225/50ZR17 front, 245/40ZR17 rear; 225/45ZR17 front, 245/40ZR17 rear

DIMENSIONS

Wheelbase, in. (mm), 1.9; 2.8; M	96.3 (2,446); 96.3 (2,446); 96.8 (2459)
Track, front, in. (mm), 1.9; 2.8; M	55.6 (1,412); 55.6 (1,412); 55.0 (1,397)
rear, in. (mm), 1.9; 2.8; M	56.2 (1,428); 58.8 (1,494); 58.7 (1,491)
Length, in. (mm)	58.5 (1,486)
Width, in. (mm), 1.9; 2.8; M	66.6 (1,692); 68.5 (1,740); 68.5 (1,740)
Height, in. (mm), 1.9; 2.8; M	50.7 (1,288); 50.7 (1,288); 49.8 (1,265)
Curb weight, lb (kg), 1,9; 2.8; M	2,690 (1,220); 2,780 (1,261); 3,085 (1,400)
Fuel tank capacity, U.S. gal. (liters)	13.5 (51.2)
Fuel economy, EPA city/highway	
5-speed manual, mpg, 1.9; 2.8; M	23/32; 19/27; 20/27

PERFORMANCE (Manufacturer's Data)

Acceleration, 0-60 mph (96 km/h), sec, 1.9; 2.8; M	8.2; 6.3; 5.5
Top speed (electronically limited)	
5-speed manual, mph (km/h), 1.9; 2.8; M	116 (187); 128 (206); 137 (221)

Mercedes-Benz SLK

The M-B SLK 230 is exactly the sort of roadster you would expect from the German *haus* sporting the 3-pointed star. It's slick looking. And it's trick. From stem to stern the SLK is chock full of the trademark engineering and technology for which the Stuttgart car builder is world famous.

When the car made its debut in 1997, it signaled yet another step in a direction change that Mercedes initiated with the new E-Class sedans. While remaining true to its tradition of quality and engineering excellence, Mercedes-Benz was trading it its *lederhosen* for Levis, Nikes and a pair

of Oakley shades. Henceforth, the M-B star also would stand for value-packed and fun-to-drive vehicles... with an attitude.

Although there's no mistaking the SLK for anything but a Mercedes, it's a huge departure from the company's typical sophisticated, solid and safe sedans. Interestingly, the SLK owes its existence to a sedan — the C-Class — upon whose chassis the SLK's platform is based. The SLK also adapts the suspension from the C-Class with twin wishbones up front and a 5-link independent setup at the rear. The car's recirculating-ball steering is also C-Class derived, but its huge disc brakes come from the considerably larger and heavier E-Class sedan.

Under the SLK's longish hood is a 2.3-liter dohc 4-cylinder that pumps out a more than healthy 185 bhp, thanks, in part, to a boost from a *Kompressor,* or as we say in the U.S., a supercharger. Compared to the naturally aspirated 2.3-liter in the C-Class sedan, the SLK motor is beefed up with a ribbed cylinder block, a stainless-steel head gasket and sodium-cooled exhaust valves. The SLK engine is intercooled to improve cylinder charging and has a broad torque curve, the max of 200 lb-ft extending from 2,500 to 4,800 rpm. Off boost, the engine sounds like a rather ordinary inline-4, but as supercharger pressure builds, it takes on a mild Banshee howl, which is especially noticeable when the engine is cold.

Despite the gated shifter, the 5-speed automatic transmission (a manual gearbox isn't offered) works best when left to its own devices — meaning place the lever in D and leave it there. The transmission's electronics are capable of "learning" the driver's driving style and adapting it to different throttle and road conditions. Perhaps it was merely a glitch in the SLK I evaluated, but I had to apply what I consider excessive throttle to get the transmission to start in 1st gear. Other times the transmission would hesitate before deciding to select 1st gear when I applied throttle after a stop.

In Europe, Mercedes offers a naturally aspirated, 136-bhp 2.0-liter 4-cylinder version available with either a manual 5-speed transmission or the 5-speed automatic. The 5-speed manual gearbox is also available on the SLK 230.

While it might be logical to assume that the "K" in the SLK name stands for Kompressor, it actually comes from the German word *Kompact,* meaning "Compact." It is certainly that, being a foot-and-a-half shorter than a C-Class and about the same overall length as a Miata. The other two-thirds of the name are only half true. The "S" for *Sportlich,* meaning sporty,

is certainly on the mark. But with a curb weight of nearly 3,000 lb, the "L" (for *Leight,* meaning Light) is a bit of a misnomer. That's nearly 700 lb more than a Miata. As for the 230 portion of the SLK's name, that's easy, it describes the engine's displacement of 2.3 liters.

Inside, the SLK is a pleasing blend of tradition and *avant garde.* A trio of classic chrome-bezeled gauges with white faces and red pointers are fitted to a dash that includes high-tech carbon fiber inserts. The rocker sill moldings are a throwback to the 1950s and the leather upholstery is timeless in its elegance and feel. The seats feature manual operation, including cushion-height adjustment. Cushions offer firm support, but I found the side bolsters a little too intrusive on my ribs unless I consciously sat in the precise middle of the seat. To further aid driver comfort, the steering wheel adjusts in/out.

The folding hardtop is both a marvel of engineering and complexity. Push forward on a center console button and five hydraulic cylinders (two for the decklid, two for the top and one for the header mechanism) hop to attention when fed by an electric-powered hydraulic pump. In a short 25 seconds the top lifts, folds and slips out of sight and into the trunk. Luggage space is less than the new Miata's but adequate for a small suitcase and a couple of oddment bags, which is pretty remarkable when you consider the amount of space the top consumes.

As with every Mercedes, safety is a key component of the new baby Benz. The SLK has both dual front airbags in the dash and side airbags in the doors. Each seat sports an integral hoop-type roll-over bar and the Mercedes passenger seat incorporates a first-of-its-kind automatic child seat recognition system which disables the passenger front airbag when the M-B accessory child seat is properly installed. The car also includes active safety features in the form of standard ABS and ASR traction control.

On the road, the SLK feels heavier than it looks. The steering is surprisingly slow, the handling is characterized by mild to moderate understeer and the Mercedes' fat Michelin Pilot radials provide excellent cornering grip. All very safe and secure. But not really sporty like a Miata. The two cars are really designed for two very different audiences. The SLK has powerful brakes and a firm but compliant ride, but it lacks the Miat's directness of response and its sense of agility. And at $40,000, it's nearly twice the price of a Miata.

SPECIFICATIONS

ENGINE

Type	dohc 16-valve inline-4, supercharged
Displacement, cc	2295

Compression ratio	8.8:1
Horsepower, bhp (kW) SAE net @ rpm	185 (138) @ 5,300
Torque, lb-ft (Nm) SAE net @ rpm	200 (270) @ 2,500
DRIVETRAIN	
Transmission	5-speed automatic
Final-drive ratio	3.27:1
CHASSIS & BODY	
Layout	front engine/rear drive
Suspension, front/rear	Unequal-length upper and lower A-arms, coil springs, tube shocks, anti-roll bar/multi-link, coil springs, tube shocks, anti-roll bar
Steering	recirculating ball, power assist
Turns, lock to lock	3.1
Brakes, front/rear	vented discs/solid discs
Wheels	16 x 7J front, 16 x 8J rear
Tires	205/55VR16 front, 225/50VR16 rear
DIMENSIONS	
Wheelbase, in. (mm)	94.5 (2,400)
Track, front, in. (mm)	55.6 (1,412)
rear, in. (mm)	58.5 (1,486)
Length, in. (mm)	157.3 (3,995)
Width, in. (mm)	67.5 (1,715)
Height, in. (mm)	50.8 (1,290)
Curb weight, lb (kg)	3,025 (1,372)
Fuel tank capacity, U.S. gal. (liters)	14.0 (53.0)
Fuel economy, EPA city/highway, mpg	22/30
PERFORMANCE (Manufacturer's Data)	
Acceleration, 0-60 mph (96 km/h), sec	7.2
Top speed, mph (km/h)	140 (225)

Porsche Boxster

This latest mid-engine Porsche is a real contradiction. In some ways it's a throwback, in other ways it represents tomorrow. The styling is certainly retro, with facial characteristics strongly reminiscent of the RSK Spyder... as well as the all-new 911. I'm a little less smitten with the rear of the car because in some ways it looks like it hasn't figured out whether it's coming or going. But two things are certain. You won't mistake the Boxster for any other car on the road, and it is instantly identifiable as a member of the proud Porsche family.

At a base price of just over $40,000, the Boxster is the latest

iteration of Porsche's entry-level sports cars represented by predecessors such as the 914 and the 924. This one is destined to enjoy far more success then either of those two earlier models because it is truly a Porsche through and through.

The Boxster's mid-engine layout is ideal for a sports car. Positioning a high percentage of the drivetrain's mass in front of the rear axle results in a low polar moment of inertia, which equates to light responsive steering, and precise directional response and turn-in. Interestingly, the Boxster platform also serves as the basis for the all new rear-engine 911.

The heart of any Porsche is its engine and the Boxster flat-6 will be instantly familiar to any Porschephile. Or will it? Although conceptually identical to the legendary 911 engine, this one is Porsche's first production, water-cooled flat-6. And it uses double-overhead cams that actuate four valves per cylinder, a feature only 911 racing engines had in the past. It's also equipped with Porsche's patented VarioCam variable intake timing, a plastic intake manifold and a pair of stainless steel headers.

Sharing only bore center spacing with its air-cooled predecessor, the Boxster engine features an aluminum alloy crankcase with cast, silicon-rich cylinder liners that are inserted during the casting process. The 7-main-bearing crankshaft and the connecting rods are made of forged steel. Despite its significant technical differences, the water-cooled Boxster flat-6 looks amazingly like the 911's air-cooled 6-cylinder. In fact, this engine serves as the basis for the 911's replacement.

Porsche engineers have cleverly tuned the Boxster's engine to produce an exhaust note similar to a 911, but muted because of the water cooling. The engine has very good flexibility at low- and mid-range speeds and revs happily to its 6,500 rpm redline. Top speed is just a tick mark less than 150 mph. With it's 5-speed gearing the Boxster feels fast, but not super quick from 0-60 mph. And shifting is not one of the Boxster's strong suits. The gearbox is a modified Audi A6 unit with cable shifting which is rather vague, especially during 4-3 downshifts.

Porsche's innovative Tiptronic automatic is a Boxster option, and if the driver chooses to operate the tranny via the steering-wheel-mounted upshift/downshift buttons, driving the automatic Boxster can be a sporting proposition.

Like the 911, the Boxster uses MacPherson struts up front and a multi-link setup at the rear. The rear suspension incorporates Porsche's Weissach rear axle which assists stability at the limit by adding a slight amount of toe-in to the outside rear wheel during hard cornering. The engineers also applied this principle up front, giving the outside front wheel a touch of toe-out under high lateral g forces.

In concert with the car's direct-acting rack-and-pinion steering and grippy Bridgestone tires, the Boxster's suspension endows the car with impressive handling, characterized by increasing amounts of mild understeer as speeds increase and also during lift-throttle conditions. Aiding the car's high-speed stability is a movable rear spoiler that Porsche claims reduces rear lift by 30 percent. It pops up at 75 mph and drops down at 50.

The Boxster's Brembo-built 4-piston aluminum monoblock brake calipers, derived from those used by the 911 GT Le Mans race car, are a production-car first, being built out of a solid one-piece casting for fade resistance to handle the most extreme high-speed Autobahn conditions. We don't encounter those types of speeds on American roads very often, but even in more normal operation these brakes are memorable for their anchor-like ability to scrub-off speed. ABS is standard and traction control is an option.

Facing the driver when he slips behind the wheel are rather traditional-looking Porsche large round gauges with one modification. The two outer gauges, speedometer on the left and combined fuel/coolant temperature gauge on the right, are overlapped by the larger central tachometer. The leather-wrapped steering wheel adjusts for reach and the seats feature power rake adjustment and manual controls for fore/aft and seat-cushion height. While the seats are wonderfully supportive, some drivers, yours truly included, find the seat backs too narrow.

The overall feel of the cockpit is one of modern functional design combined with an over-abundance of hard plastic. There is no softness to the Boxster interior and the excessive use of shiny black plastic for switches, buttons and stalks results in annoying glare under some light conditions.

Operating the roadster's fabric top is a model of simplicity: Twist one windshield header latch, then push one button and the power-operated top disappears under a trap door behind the cockpit. Some of the convertible-top brackets are fabricated from magnesium to reduce weight. This is just one of several weight-cutting measures Porsche engineers implemented. For instance, the suspension arms, brake calipers and hubs are cast aluminum, reducing unsprung weight. As a result, the Boxster, while longer and wider than the current 911, is actually 300 pound lighter.

While entry-level in concept, the Boxster is not entry-level to own. Clever marketing has fixed the base price at just over $40,000, but that's without a wide variety of options that most Porsche drivers will not want. Adding items such as the optional sport suspension package and several comfort and convenience features, will have many Boxster out-the-door price tags pushing 50. That certainly pushes the affordability of the car well beyond that of the typical Miata buyer.

SPECIFICATIONS

ENGINE

Type	dohc 16-valve flat-6
Displacement, cc	2480
Compression ratio	11.0:1
Horsepower, bhp (kW) SAE net @ rpm	201 (150) @ 6,000
Torque, lb-ft (Nm) SAE net @ rpm	181 (244) @ 4,500

DRIVETRAIN

Transmission	5-speed manual, optional Tiptronic automatic
Final-drive ratio	3.89:1, 5-speed; 4.21:1, Tiptronic

CHASSIS & BODY

Layout	mid engine/rear drive
Suspension, front/rear	MacPherson struts, lower A-arms, coil springs, tube shocks, anti-roll bar/Chapman struts, lower lateral links, trailing links, toe links, coil springs, tube shocks, anti-roll bar
Steering	recirculating ball, power assist
Turns, lock to lock	3.0
Brakes, front/rear	vented discs/vented discs
Wheels	16 x 6J front, 16 x 7J rear
Tires	205/55ZR16 front, 225/50ZR16 rear

DIMENSIONS

Wheelbase, in. (mm)	95.2 (2,418)
Track, front, in. (mm)	57.7 (1,466)
rear, in. (mm)	60.2 (1,529)
Length, in. (mm)	171.0 (4,343)
Width, in. (mm)	70.1 (1,781)
Height, in. (mm)	50.8 (1,290)
Curb weight, lb (kg)	5-speed: 2,820 (1,279); Tiptronic: 2,955 (1,340)
Fuel tank capacity, U.S. gal (liters)	15.3 (58.0)
Fuel economy, EPA city/highway, mpg	19/26, 5-speed; 17/24, Tiptronic

PERFORMANCE (Manufacturer's Data)

Acceleration, 0-60 mph (96 km/h), sec	5-speed: 6.75; Tiptoronic: 7.4
Top speed, mph (km)	5-speed: 149 (240); Tiptpronic: 146 (235)

Rover MGF

Britain's Rover Group began its sports car program in 1989. MGF project manager Nick Fell says, "1989 was an important year; that was the year Mazda launched the MX-5 Miata. I think, if we were really honest, the European industry would recognize that Mazda saw a market opportunity and seized it, creating a sports car, the likes of which had traditionally came from Europe, and particular England. And our work was, partly anyway, to reclaim our own territory."

Thus Rover started its sports car project, appropriately and somehow dramatically called "Phoenix."

The Rover team investigated three small sports car configurations: front-wheel-drive; front-engine, rear-wheel-drive; and midship-engine. They were called Phoenix Route 1, 2 and 3, or PR1, 2 and 3, respectively. The process was quite similar to what Mazda had done when the MX-5 was conceived in the mid-Eighties. For this first new design in 32 years (the MGB was the last one), Rover chose the PR3 mid-engine configuration on its dynamic merits. Affordability, a critical issue, was handled through the use of an existing front-wheel-drive power train and chassis components. Interestingly, Rover's early concept and package engineering event displayed three cars for comparison purposes: PR3, MX-5 and MGB.

The MGF's styling is modern and British, neatly avoiding a pitfall of going retro and not so much emphasizing it's a midship-engine car. There are unmistakable styling cues such as a grille split by a large octagonal emblem in a shield. The racy filler cap is a nice touch insisted upon by the designer. The interior is quite spacious with a symmetrical dashboard, again with an embossed octagon on the top, on the dual-cockpit theme. The seats are less bucket than some of the car's competitors, here its every-day character shows up.

Rover's K-series 1.4/1.6-liter 4-cylinder engine was enlarged to 1.8-liters, employing the clever "damp liner" construction in its aluminum cylinder block. The high-power version is fitted with an equally ingenious, albeit complex, variable valve system, VVC, which continuously varies the intake valve duration from 220 to 295 degrees.

The 5-speed manual transmission is from Rover's front-wheel-drive cars, jointly developed with Honda, and is shifted via cables. Shift effort is slightly heavier and the lever travel longer than that of the similarly configured Toyota MR2, but is quite positive in its feel.

Suspension is by double-wishbones combined with Hydragas units. Hydragas is an interconnected suspension system employing fluid and gas, for pitch control and to produce a variable spring rate. Its application to the MGF is a significant advantage because the difference in weight between lightly and fully loaded conditions is smaller than, say, a 4-passenger car. Hydragas' relatively small travel (150 mm versus the first-generation Miata's 170 mm) functions more satisfactorily under these conditions. Unlike earlier Rover Hydragas cars, the MGF is fitted with tubular shock absorbers and stabilizer (anti-roll) bars, clearly separating the various suspension functions such as roll control, damping and pitch control.

The MGF's chassis is tuned to satisfy those times when the car has to behave like an "everyday sports car," combining good roll control, stable understeer, and above all quite an exceptional ride for a sports car of this size. Roadholding is very good, however, handling may not feel as crisp as the MX-5's, owing largely to its electric power steering, which is not as linear or natural in its assistance.

The all-steel, welded box shell is very rigid, thanks to deep side sills and a hefty box-section member under the seats. The latter, however, results in a high, awkward driving position, hardly helped by the non-adjusting steering wheel. The Pinninfarina-engineered soft top is easy to operate and stores neatly under a tonneau. Wind buffeting is minimal because of the high rear deck which prevents air blowing back.

The MGF is an endearing open sports car which has the honor of being the only affordable mid-engine sports car, until, perhaps, joined by Toyota's re-entry in the lightweight arena with the MR-S.

SPECIFICATIONS

ENGINE

Type	dohc 16-valve inline-4; high-power version is fitted with VVC variable valve duration system
Displacement, cc	1796
Compression ratio	10.5:1
Horsepower, 1.8i, bhp (kW) SAE net @ rpm	120 (89) @ 5,500
1.8i VVC, bhp (kW) SAE net @ rpm	143 (107) @ 7,000
Max torque, 1.8i, lb-ft (Nm) SAE net @ rpm	122 (165) @ 3,000
1.8i VVC, lb-ft (Nm) SAE net @ rpm	128 (174) @ 4,500

DRIVETRAIN

Transmission	5-speed manual
Final-drive ratio, 1.8i; 1.8i VVC	3.938:1; 4.200:1

CHASSIS AND BODY

Layout	mid-engine/rear drive

Suspension, front and rear	Unequal-length upper and lower A-arms, Hydragas inter-connected spring/damper units, tube shocks, anti-roll bars
Steering	rack & pinion, electrically assisted, speed-sensitive
Turns, lock to lock	3.1
Brakes, front/rear	vented discs/solid discs; ABS optional
Wheels	15 x 6J; 6-spoke alloy
Tires	185/55VR15 front, 205/50VR15 rear

DIMENSIONS

Wheelbase, in. (mm)	93.5 (2,375)
Tracks, front, in. (mm)	55.1 (1,400)
rear, in. (mm)	55.5 (1,410)
Length, in. (mm)	154.1 (3,910)
Width, in. (mm)	64.0 (1628)
Height, in. (mm)	49.6 (1,260)
Weight, lb (kg), 1.8i; 1.8i VVC	2,337 (1,060); 2,359 (1,070)
Fuel tank capacity, U.S. gal. (liters)	13.2 (50.0)

PERFORMANCE 1.8i

Acceleration, 0-60 mph, sec, 1.8i; 1.8i VVC	8.5; 7.0
Max speed, mph (km/h), 1.8i; 1.8i VVC	120 (193); 130 (209)
Fuel consumption, European urban, mpg (liters/100 km)	8.4 (28.0); 9.3 (25.3)

Fiat Barchetta

Fiat's Barchetta is a front-wheel-drive roadster, and as such it may not be what the die-hard enthusiast would consider the classic approach toward a proper sports car. But sports car it is, as the roadster is full of life and fun. And it's very Italian to its core, from the pretty exterior to the daring interior.

The Barchetta is based on the small front-wheel-drive Punto hatchback platform and Bravo running gear, fitted with a zippy twin-cam, 16-valve 1747-cc inline 4-cylinder engine putting out 130 bhp at 6,300 rpm and 121 lb-ft torque at 4,300 rpm.

Rowing through five crisp cogs, the Barchetta feels busier than its competitors. The raucous exhaust note makes it feel and sound fast, but it's not as quick as the Miata. Nevertheless, it's a bundle of fun. The engine really gets on "cam" above 4,000 rpm.

The Barchetta's suspension is by front MacPherson struts and rear trailing arms with coil springs, tubular shocks and stabilizer (anti-roll) bars at either end, a typical European fwd arrangement. The car's response to the driver's command is quick and precise, its power assisted rack-and-pinion steering requiring only 2.5 turns from lock to lock. With terminal understeer under a heavy foot, there's no mistaking the Barchetta is a front-wheel-drive car. However, the understeer switches to an abrupt oversteer on lift off. At higher velocities on bumpy corners, its rear-end becomes a bit twitchy. But that only happens at the limit, and the car makes you accept all that behavior as part of the fun.

There are some rough edges in fit and finish, but the car's sexy styling and great cockpit make up for them. The interior is really dramatically styled, with body-color panels running along the lower dash and on the door trims, imparting an impression that you are really in a steel, not plastic automobile (actually these panels are plastic.) The soft top is stored under a hard tonneau cover, but the arrangement is a bit awkward to handle, another typical Italian trait.

SPECIFICATIONS

ENGINE

Type	dohc 16-valve inline-4, transversely mounted
Displacement, cc	1747
Compression ratio	10.3:1
Horse power, bhp (kW) SAE net @ rpm	130 (97) DIN @ 6,300
Torque, lb-ft, (Nm) SAE net @ rpm	123 (164) DIN @ 4,300

DRIVETRAIN

Transmission	5-speed manual gearbox
Final-drive ratio	3.563:1

CHASSIS AND BODY

Layout	front engine/front drive
Suspension, front/rear	MacPherson struts, coil springs, tube shoks, anti-roll bar/trailing arms, coil springs, tube shocks, anti-roll bar.
Steering	rack & pinion, power assisted
Turns lock to lock	2.4
Brakes, front/rear	ventilated discs/drums; ABS.
Wheels	15 x 6J, alloy
Tires	195/55R15

DIMENSIONS

Wheelbase, in. (mm)	90.0 (2,275)
Track, front, in. (mm)	55.1 (1,400)
rear, in. (mm)	55.5 (1,410)
Length, in. (mm)	154.1 (3,910)
Width, in. (mm)	69.3 (1,768)
Height, in. (mm)	49.6 (1,260)
Curb weight, lb (kg)	2,398 (1,090)
Fuel tank capacity, U.S. gal. (liters)	13.2 (50.0)
Weight, lb (kg)	2,398 (1,090)

PUBLICATION STAFF

Editor	Koichi Yazaki
Editorial Staff	Syuki Hanaoka
	Akishige Mitsui
	Takuji Maeno
	Naoto Nakamura
Design and Layout	Tsutomu Yamashita
	RING Ltd.
Staff Photographer	Maki Saito
Cover and Photo Essey	Kohmei Hanaoka
Driving Impressions	Guy Spangenberg
Photographic Sources	Bigstone
	Mazda Motor Corporation
	MAZDASPEED
	Yoshihiko Okamoto
	Susumu Okano
	Roadster Club of Japan
	Jack K. Yamagichi
	Koichi Yazaki
Special Thanks	Hotel Highland Resort
	Hotel Nishinagato Resort
	PRESTIGE CO., LTD.